Colonial and Historic Homes of Maryland

COLONIAL AND HISTORIC HOMES OF MARYLAND

ETCHINGS BY DON SWANN Text by Don Swann, Jr.

Foreword by F. Scott Fitzgerald

The Johns Hopkins University Press
Baltimore and London

To Don Swann, Sr., a great artist and a loving father who will never be forgotten, and to all Marylanders who contributed to the first 350 years of our state's heritage.

Colonial and Historic Homes of Maryland was first published privately, in 1939, in a two-volume set limited to 200 copies. In 1975, the Johns Hopkins University Press reproduced in one volume the 100 etchings of the original edition and the text that accompanied them. In 1983, Liberty Publishing Company, of Cockeysville, Maryland, issued a paperback edition that updated the original text. The 1983 edition is reprinted here.

The Johns Hopkins University Press
701 West 40th Street, Baltimore, Maryland 21211-2190
The Johns Hopkins Press Ltd., London

The paper in this book meets the standard requirements of American National Standard for Information Sciences— Permanence of Paper for Printed Library Materials, ANSI Z39.48-1984.

Library of Congress Cataloging-in-Publication Data

Swann, Don, 1889–1954.
    Colonial and historic homes of Maryland / etchings by
  Don Swann ; text by Don Swann, Jr. ; foreword by
  F. Scott Fitzgerald.
        p.   cm.
    Reprint. Originally published: Baltimore : Etchcrafters Art
  Guild, 1939.
    Includes index.
    ISBN 0-8018-4247-6
    1. Dwellings—Maryland. 2. Historic buildings—Maryland.
  3. Maryland—Biography. 4. Maryland—History, Local.
  5. Architecture, Domestic—Maryland—Pictorial works.
  6. Architecture, Colonial—Maryland—Pictorial works. I. Swann,
  Don, 1911– . II. Title.
  F182.S93   1991
  769.92—dc20   90-28979

CONTENTS

FOREWORD

The undersigned can only consider himself a native of the Maryland Free State through ancestry and adoption. But the impression of the fames and the domains, the vistas and the glories of Maryland followed many a young man West after the Civil War and my father was of that number. Much of my early childhood in Minnesota was spent in asking him such questions as:

"—and how long did it take Early's column to pass Glenmary that day?" (That was a farm in Montgomery County.)

and:

"—what would have happened if Jeb Stewart's cavalry had joined Lee instead of raiding all the way to Rockville?"

and:

—tell me again about how you used to ride through the woods with a spy up behind you on the horse."

or:

"Why wouldn't they let Francis Scott Key off the British frigate?" And since so many legends of my family went west with father, memories of names that go back before Braddock's disaster such as Caleb Godwin of Hockley-in-ye-Hole, or Philip Key of Tudor Hall, or Pleasance Ridgeley—so there must be hundreds and hundreds of families in such an old state whose ancestral memories are richer and fuller than mine.

But time obliterates people and memories and only the more fortunate landmarks survive. In the case of this fine book, it is upon the home above all that Don Swann has concentrated his talents and his painstaking research—the four walls (or sixteen as it may be) of Baronial Maryland, or the artistic result of the toil and sweat that some forever anonymous craftsman put into a balcony or a parquet. And outside this general range, the etcher has also paused here and there to jot down some detail of plainer houses that helps to make this a permanent record of the history of the Free State.

His work, naturally, will speak for itself, and, to allow it to do so, I cut short this prelude with the expression of high hopes for this venture by one of the State's adopted sons.

Francis Scott Key Fitzgerald

PREFACE

The Colonial dwellings of Maryland, rich in historical associations and mellowed by time's handling, stand mute reminders of our traditions of gracious living and a legendary past. Others have described and tabulated, recorded and waxed lyrical, through the medium of the written word. This has been done. My efforts have been in another direction, although motivated by kindred ideals—the preservation for posterity of a glamorous past and a cultural inheritance.

With the eyes of an artist, through the medium of an etcher's needle, I have endeavored to capture the picturesque on a copper plate. The quaint charm of primitive cabins, the rugged appeal of sturdy farm houses, the gracious air of commodious manor homes, and the impelling respect inspired by palatial mansions of great land-owners prompted me to give of my best in this hitherto unadventured field.

To record accurately architectural masses and embellishments while retaining an agreeable picture; to allow free rein to the etcher's technique, trying for methods, ingenuity, and subtlety that might give variety and yet maintain the quality of a fine print; this was the task I set myself.

The patient peruser of these pages will see an example of dry-point in the Ridout House. Oldfield's Point is rendered in soft ground. Aquatone is shown in Mount Clare and Glasgow. A special technique, styled sugar plate, is exemplified in the Drane House. All through the work are plates that have touches, here and there, of glass brush work done through the ground while the plate was in the acid bath. The foreground of Snow Hill is made in this way.

The large majority of the plates are etched in a straightforward manner, with about six to twelve stop-outs. Few corrections were made. A rag wipe, with a touch of the hand occasionally, were the sole devices used in printing.

Baltimore
1939

Colonial and Historic Homes of Maryland

BARD'S FIELDS

Curley's Road, Ridge

About three miles from Scotland, near Calvert's Rest, at the head of an unnamed inlet with Harry James Creek on the South, stands a small frame house with four brick chimneys. The place has three names, of which the best known is Bard's Fields. However, it also is referred to as Gray's Neck and Barred Fields. The house at one time was occupied by the Loker family for many years, as the tombstones in a field at the back testify. In 1909, the property was acquired by George W. Pratt, the father of the present owner, Mr. James Pratt. Currently, the house is not occupied, though Mr. Pratt has installed a new roof. The Pratts built their own house on the same farm property where Bard's Fields stands.

Bard's Fields, one-and-a-half storeys in height and but two small rooms wide, is not pretentious. There are no dormer windows looking over the small inlet only a few hundred feet from the steps leading to the front porch.

Weather beaten clapboards cover the brick nogging. The foundation is of brick. Twin double chimneys rise from either end of the house, having a brick pent between them and hugging the wall closely, square and business-like, for use and not for ornament.

The worn shingles of the sloping roof added to the impression of age which the appearance of the dwelling does nothing to belie. H and HL hinges are on some of the doors and pegs hold the rafters together. Within a foot and a half of the pent line of the roof there is a peculiar little opening known as a "lie-on-your-stomach window."

From the general aspect of the place and the tombstones in the small graveyard, it would seem that this house must have been built some time in the middle of the eighteenth century. The construction seems to warrant such a date and the apparent age of the bricks to confirm it.

The rooms are small and low with a single window lighting each of them. The narrow hall runs through to the back where there is an overhang supported by poles. There is a narrow winding staircase leading to the attic-like second floor and a ladder to the garret.

The Loker family at one time was one of the wealthiest and most important in St. Mary's County. Mulberry Fields and Woodlawn, both now in other hands, were also once their property.

Another of the smaller homes worthy of note in St. Mary's County is Resurrection Manor, or Scotch Neck. This early brick dwelling overlooking the Patuxent River was built by Captain Thomas Cornwaleys in 1653. The manor was later in the possession of George Plowden, son of Sir Edmund Plowden, Earl of Albion.

BATCHELOR'S HOPE

Manor Road, Chaptico

Almost in the middle of the top of the neck formed by the Wicomico River and St. Clement's Bay, is Batchelor's Hope, standing on a slight rise a half mile from the town of Hurry. The fifteen hundred acres of "Bashford Manor," on which the house is situated, were surveyed in 1650 for Dr. Thomas Gerrard.

Dr. Gerrard sold the property to Governor Thomas Notley in either 1667 or 1678, according to the Joshua Doyne Patent of 1683. Notley placed Batchelor's Hope in the possession of Col. Benjamin Rozier who lived there with his wife, Ann Sewall and their son Notley Rozier, until Notley's death in 1679.

By will Batchelor's Hope was devised to Benjamin Rozier and Charles Calvert, the Third Lord Baltimore. Baltimore bought Rozier's share and in 1683 patented it to Joshua Doyne. The Doyne family owned it until 1753 when William Hammersley's name appears on the Rent Rolls as owning Batchelor's Hope. After his death, his son Francis sold it to James Edgerton (1796).

Edgerton died in 1811. Various members of the Turner family were owners until Dr. John Turner's death in 1883. In 1884, Col. Miles acquired the property and by will, devised it to Josephine Garner, his great granddaughter. She married Truman Slingluff and in 1937 sold Batchelor's Hope to Col. and Mrs. Walter L. Simpson. In 1975, The National Trust for Historic Preservation accepted Batchelor's Hope, a Historic House, as a gift from the Simpsons who retained the right of occupancy during their life time.

The house is believed to have been built in 1668. It is a type of dwelling said to be unique in America.

The building is of brick with a two storey central section and single storey flanking wings. The portico is inset, as is that of Tudor Hall in Leonardtown. This is unusual in Colonial architecture. The front door opens directly into the hunt room, which is panelled and has a large fireplace on the left, flanked on either side by built-in cupboards with butterfly shelves. On the far right is the door to a small office with a fireplace. Another door, opposite, on the far left of the hunt room, opens into a bedroom. Here there is a corner fireplace with beautiful panelling to the ceiling. This room is balanced by another bedroom, a little larger, with the same type of mantel arrangement. There is a second door in this room which leads to the portico. Across the portico, passing the steps, is the dining room, with a fireplace on the left and a cupboard beyond it. The kitchen quarters extend from this room. The plan of the lodge is amazingly compact and simple.

The stairway to the two bed chambers on the second floor is so arranged that the second storey can be gained without going into the lower part of the house.

One of the most attractive features of Batchelor's Hope is the fine brick work of glazed green and purple tinted Flemish bond, scarcely dimmed by time. A quarter-round base, a frieze of alternate rosettes and triglyphs over the portico, and carved endboards on the cornices add decoration to the front of the house.

CREMONA

Cremona Road, Mechanicsville

Cremona, named after the city of Cremona, Italy, where Stradivarius Amati and others made fine violins, is situated on the Patuxent River between De La Brooke and Trent Hall. By land, it is approached by Cremona Road, off Route 6. The house is a long two-and-a-half storey brick building, without dormer windows. When constructed in 1819 by Dr. John Thomas, a dedicated amateur violinist born at nearby De La Brooke, the mansion had only one wing. The left addition was made by General and Mrs. Howard C. Davidson, in 1930, when they required a modern kitchen. However, this wing was carefully built to conform with the original, as it is the same size and is composed of bricks taken from partitions removed from the central part of the house. Cremona has four enormous chimneys on its central section, with a chimney on each of the smaller flanking wings.

The slave kitchen contains a beautifully decorated and very large fireplace measuring four feet high, seven feet wide, and five feet deep, built out into the room. Had Confederate soldiers wished to hide, this chimney would have gulped up at least ten of the burliest greyclads in the South. The original ceiling beams and two-foot wide boards can be seen as they have been left uncovered by the Davidsons in the restoration work.

The arrangement of the building is symmetrical. A porch shades the wide front door which has an oval fan-light above it. This gives on the spacious hallway running the depth of the house to a door matching the one on the land side and opening on a lawn, beyond which the river stretches a mile and a half across to Calvert County. Rising on the left of the hall, a third of the way down, is one of the most remarkable hanging staircases in Maryland, and indeed, the entire coun-try. The first flight ascends half way to the second floor to a landing which covers the width of the hall like a bridge. Here the stairs divide and reach the second floor in twin flights. This arrangement is repeated to gain the peaked attic, which has been transformed into comfortable bedrooms. The banisters are of maple, carefully colored by dirt ground in by hand. The risers are of virgin pine, as is all the flooring.

The house originally had no panelling of any kind except a chair rail in the dining room, but now there is a small library, opening off the hall at the foot of the stairs, panelled from floor to ceiling with wood taken from a Colonial home in Baltimore. On the same side of the hall, farther down, is the dining room beautified by a fine mantel and antique furniture. Indeed, the whole house is filled with museum pieces. The right side of the dwelling, originally made up of two rooms, has been thrown into one large, well-lighted living room running the full depth of the building.

Cremona is famous for its boxwood and other gardens which lie to the right of the house. Here is no attempt to ape the ornamental grounds of the great English homes, but a fine informality, well suited to the atmosphere of the mansion, reigns. A modern swimming pool nestles in shrubbery, beyond which is another garden and the greenhouse. The 900-acre estate lies on the shore of the Patuxent River, which in 1933 almost washed Cremona down into the Chesapeake Bay, and is bounded to the north by Persimmon Creek and to the south by Cremona and Mud Creeks.

Since 1966, Cremona has been owned and occupied by Dr. Norton Dodge and his wife, Nancy. Dr. Dodge is on the faculty of St. Mary's College of Maryland at St. Mary's City.

CROSS MANOR

Villa Road, St. Inigoe's

On St. Inigoe's Creek, a few miles from St. Mary's City, stands Cross Manor, reputed to be the oldest brick house in Maryland. It was built by Thomas Cornwaleys, a fine soldier, gallant sailor, and good friend and one of the commissioners of Leonard Calvert, the first Governor of Colonial Maryland. Most likely, John Robinson, an indentured carpenter and bricklayer brought over from England by Cornwaleys, did the actual construction of Cross Manor. The building was completed sometime between 1642 and 1644, since a year later the owner lodged a complaint saying that certain valuables had been stolen from his dwelling.

The unpretentious two-and-a-half storey stone manor house stands close to the creek and is almost hidden by large shade trees and high boxwood. Its outlines have been changed from time to time; the roof has been raised from a gambrel to a gable shape, and dormer windows have been added. This was probably accomplished sometime around 1800, at the time when Mordecai Jones acquired the house from his father-in-law, James Bisco, Jr., to accommodate his large family.

The front door is directly in line with the back entrance and gives on a hall. On the right hand side halfway down rises a beautiful staircase. On the opposite side of the hall are doors which lead to the dining room and the parlor, where the furnishings are of the finest type to be found. Dark stained panelling imparts an atmosphere of dignity and charm to the hall.

The origin of the name, Cross Manor, is not established, but legend offers two explanations. It has been said that a number of Virginians were killed by Indians while exploring St. Inigoe's Creek and a marker in the shape of a cross was erected where their bodies were found. From this cross, it is said, Thomas Cornwaleys got the name for his home when he decided, after having first built a water mill, "to build a house to put my head in."

Another and more romantic tale has it that a later Cornwaleys accidently shot and killed a very dear friend while hunting. He left home and became wealthy but could never forget his tragic deed. Haunted by this memory, he returned to his ancestral home, placed a cross where his friend died, and built a small house nearby, in which he remained a recluse for the rest of his days.

Thomas Cornwaleys won the first Colonial naval engagement to take place in Maryland waters. He captured the boat of William Claiborne, who had been indulging in some privateering in the forbidden waters of the Chesapeake. It was probably a result of that victory that Cornwaleys was appointed deputy Governor for the colony. The Manor of Cornwaleys Cross was patented to Thomas Cornwaleys on September 8, 1638.

From the death of Thomas Cornwaleys until Dr. Caleb M. Jones came into possession of the property in the late eighteenth century, there is some question as to when various owners actually held the property. Following Dr. Jones' ownership, Cross Manor belonged to the sisters of Captain Randolph Jones, Elvira Ann Jones Ellicott and Emily Regina Jones. Elvira was married to James Fox Ellicott of Baltimore City. From them, the manor descended in direct line to Mrs. Charles Sterett Grason, whose daughters Mary Louise Grason Manning Cruit and Dorothy Sterett Grason inherited the property when she died. Mary Louise and Dorothy lived at Cross Manor all of their lives. The present owners are Mr. and Mrs. Eugene Guy Rea. Mrs. Rea, the former Mrs. Charles Glendower Ellicott has two sons, Roderick Denning Ellicott and John Glendower Ellicott, who are the twelfth generation of the bloodline to live at Cross Manor.

CUTHBERT'S FORTUNE

Three Notch Road, Hollywood

Midway between the small towns of Hillville and Hollywood on the Three Notch Road, in St. Mary's County, is a short lane leading to the site of the quaint and charming little one-and-a-half storey frame house known as Cuthbert's Fortune, or Industry. The house was built by Jessop Floyd early in the nineteenth century. There was a lumber mill in the neighborhood run by this early Floyd which would account for the name Industry, and Cuthbert's Fortune must have been derived from "St. Cuthbert's Manor."

The house remained in the Floyd family until it burned in 1951, soon after the death of Miss Lucy R. Floyd, last owner, granddaughter of the builder, and second cousin of Miss Olivia Floyd of Rose Hill and War Between the States fame. The land has since been re-developed.

Cuthbert's Fortune had no cellar. The extremely steep pitched roof was a rather remarkable architectural feature, as most of the houses in this region have a hip roof or a gentle slope. Twin brick chimneys, rising from the southern end of the house, barely cleared the ridge. Between the chimneys was a small brick pent with a little window.

To the right of the house proper was a slave kitchen connected to the main house by what would be known on the Eastern Shore as the colonnade. Inside this annex there was an enormous fireplace about which the slaves used to gather on cold winter nights. Reminiscent of succulent feasts were the curious long-handled frying pans which leaned against the blackened bricks. A huge iron pot sat comfortably in a dark corner.

The main part of the house was entered on the extreme left, where a hall ran from front to back. The stairs to the second storey rose on the left side of the hall against the outside wall, while two doors opened on the right. The first door led to the parlor with its plain manteled fireplace. The other hall door led to the dining room, out of which the door to the kitchen passage-way opened. This room also had a plain mantel of the same type as that in the parlor.

Everywhere there were evidences of handicraft. The large beams supporting the ceiling still had the original axe marks on them and were morticed together. The spindles in the balustrade of the simple staircase were uneven, as if there had been trouble in getting them to match. In the small garden in front of the house were two box trees about fourteen feet high.

This was the house of a holder of a small property in contrast to the stately brick dwellings of the wealthy. It was more of a home and less the grand landed estate with its manor rights and two thousand acres. Its building marked the beginning of a new age and was the first note that the small owner rather than the great landed proprietor would survive as the farmer of Maryland.

DE LA BROOKE

De La Brooke Road, Mechanicsville

In the year 1650, Robert Brooke arrived in Maryland from England, accompanied by his wife and ten children, twenty-eight other persons, and a pack of hounds. He settled about fifteen miles up the Patuxent River, the first to do so in these parts. He achieved the distinctions of being appointed Commander of the newly erected Charles County, and Acting Governor of the Province in 1652. De La Brooke was his original grant, and a few years later it was turned into a manor of two thousand acres, with Baker Brooke, his oldest son, as Lord of the Manor. The original house, torn down by George Thomas in 1835, stood on the top of a hill about a mile from the river. It was in this house that the Provisional Council of Maryland met with Governor Charles Calvert on July 19, 1662.

The present dwelling was built in 1830 by George Thomas at the edge of the river, so close that one can almost step from a boat to the back porch. De La Brooke is of brick made on the property and its four large chimneys are a landmark along the river. The house is two-and-a-half storeys high with a large basement and a small kitchen wing with a large chimney on the right. The grounds are well kept and tall trees cast a welcome shadow on the front of the building, while the large verandah at the back shades the river side of the house and provides a cool place to rest on hot summer afternoons.

De La Brooke is entered from a small porch which is gained by a flight of six wooden steps. The main wing is almost square, with a hall running from front to back on the extreme left. The stairs, not pretentious, rise on this side next to the outside wall. However, their very plainness has a beauty which many of the older and more self-conscious manors fail to achieve by mere ornateness.

The estate of De La Brooke is rich in historical interest. Baker Brooke became Surveyor General of the Province and married a niece of the second Lord Baltimore. He died in 1678, leaving the property to his daughter, Ann Brooke, who married Benedict Leonard Boarman. Richard Basil Boarman inherited it in 1757 and in turn left the manor to his daughter, Catherine Brooke Boarman, who was married to Major William Thomas Jr. A son was born on March 11, 1785, and christened James. He became the twenty-sixth Governor of Maryland, serving from 1833 to 1835.

In 1813, one year before the British expedition sailed past De La Brooke, to land at Benedict and march on Washington, Major Thomas died, and was succeeded by his son, George. The year 1856 marked his death, and the property passed to Dr. James Thomas, his son. Dr. Thomas died October 18, 1892. The last Thomas to own the manor house and eighth direct descendant of Robert Brooke, Clarence Wood Thomas of Charlotte Hall, Maryland, sold De La Brooke to Mr. Leander-McCormick-Goodhart, of the British Embassy. He had used the house for a ducking lodge and summer home, as the pages of the visitors book abundantly testify. His widow is the present owner.

LONG LANE FARM

Hermanville Road, Lexington Park

On the shore of the Chesapeake Bay, at the end of a long road from which the farm gets its name, stands the shell of Long Lane Farm, a small one-and-a-half storey house, with brick ends joined by clapboards. Its pent line was flattened at either end in the English manner. On the western end there are twin outside chimneys, on the eastern end but one. Two dormer windows once looked out over the Chesapeake Bay; under these was the porch joined to the roof in one long sweep of shingles.

The house was built before 1674, as it was then that its owner, Lieutenant Colonel John Jarboe of Dijon, High Sheriff of St. Mary's County, died. Later Long Lane Farm came into the possession of the Carrolls, and in 1915 into the hands of Marcel Longini, formerly of Chicago, then a resident of Baltimore. In April, 1938, he sold the property to Martin Kohn of Baltimore. The present owner of the property is Larry Millison.

The original plan of the house provided for only two rooms but two more were added later. Contrary to custom, the walls were not very thick, the heaviest being only nine inches except around the chimneys. The front door was gained, in days gone by, from a brick terrace, although in the later years one entered from the porch immediately into a seventeen-foot-square living room with a boxed-in corner staircase on the right, leading to the upper floor. The partition wall between the front room and the kitchen was on the left, with a door in the middle. Daylight entered through the one window next to the door. During the winter this room was very dark. None of the rooms on the lower floor had more than a single window.

Directly in line with the front entrance was the rear door, reached by a short hall separating the two twelve-foot-square back rooms. From the room on the left of the hall there was a door to a long narrow cupboard along one side of the bedchamber. Tradition says that this was the last refuge in the event that the enemy succeeded in capturing the rest of the house. However, in modern times it was used as a jam and preserve cupboard. Alas, for the high romance of yesteryear!

Upstairs, the rooms were small and the roof sloped down toward the side walls, giving them a feeling of intimacy. Each room had its own fireplace, except for one room downstairs.

The cellar was entered from the outside through a large arched opening. In it arches were seen again, for an arch supported each first floor fireplace, at the same time conserving bricks. A quaint note was added by the square brick smokehouse where could be seen the original hand-wrought meat racks on which great hams were preserved for long winter months.

In 1972, a tragic fire completely gutted the inside of Long Lane Farm. Fortunately, the mantels had been previously removed to another house. Mr. Millison acquired the property in 1980, with the intention of developing it. His hope is to preserve part of the old house and fence it in, along with a marker and some photographs of how it once stood. If this were not feasible, the shell would have to undergo demolition, a sad fate indeed.

MULBERRY FIELDS

Route 244, Leonardtown

In the village of Valley Lee there stands a five-bay mid-Georgian brick building with a hipped roof, similar to contemporary Tidewater Virginia buildings, and known as Mulberry Fields. It is the only example of this type of domestic architecture in St. Mary's County. Both porches and the kitchen wing are later additions. A dairy, meathouse, kitchen and workhouse, built later than the main house, are placed symmetrically north of it, forming a rectangular court. The kitchen garden and bowling green are situated north of the court, separated by a row of large boxwood. The kitchen and the workhouse have substantial brick dependencies built in the late Georgian style as replacements of frame structures. These were built at the turn of the 19th century. The second floor of each apparently housed a slave family and offered more comfortable living quarters than the usual log houses occupied by most slaves.

From the south facade of Mulberry Fields the mile long "Avenue Field", lined on either side with trees, stretches to the Potomac River. An 18th century owner planted the rows in an ever-widening angle from the house to create the illusion of two parallel rows continuing to the river.

The center hall, great room and dining room are panelled to the ceiling, making it one of the most completely panelled houses in Maryland.

After John Attaway Clarke bought the 25-acre tract, he or his brother-in-law, John Somerville, may have built the mansion in 1755. The plantation reached the height of its prosperity around 1800 in the tenure of John's son, William Somerville. Shortly before his death, he increased his holdings to 10,000 acres along the Potomac, and his slave labor force from 46 to 180 by 1806. Most of these worked in the fields, cultivating tobacco, corn, wheat, flax, and cotton. Somerville owned an early patent cotton gin and a fabric mill. Cooks, stablehands and housekeepers gave the mansion and outbuildings the appearance of a busy village. Most of these outbuildings have since disappeared.

Inside the house, the rooms were comfortable and somewhat over-furnished with the accumulations of two prosperous generations of Clarkes and Somervilles and heirlooms from different branches of the family.

William Somerville died in 1806. He had no will, so the Orphan's Court distributed the property to his children, all of whom were minors at the time. During the War of 1812, the three got together and attempted to sell the property, due to its proximity to the water and the continuing enemy action. They had no buyers. The new master, William Clarke Somerville, was a romantic cosmopolitan figure. An army major, he fought in Venezuela under Simon Bolivar and in the War of 1812. He made the grand tour of Europe, meeting Lord Byron, the Duke of Wellington and Lucien Bonaparte, among others. Upon returning from Italy, he rechristened Mulberry Fields as Montalbino. While gambling with local gentry, he won Sotterley.

In 1822, when he sold Mulberry Fields, he purchased Stratford Hall across the Potomac, the birthplace of Robert E. Lee. His friendship with President John Quincy Adams led to a diplomatic post in Greece. Enroute, on board a ship to France with Marquis de Lafayette, he contracted a fatal illness and died. He was buried on Lafayette's estate.

The property then passed quickly through several hands until Thomas Loker acquired it in 1832. The Lokers sold it to Jessie Lennox Fay and Colonel William Garlan Fay in 1916. The present owners, Mary Lennox Jansson and Holger B. Jannson, purchased it in 1958. It is still worked as a plantation of about 600 acres, with tobacco remaining the main cash crop.

ST. MICHAEL'S MANOR

Route 5, Scotland

In St. Mary's County, a mile from Scotland and a mile and a half from Point Lookout, just off the main road near the water of a small inlet from the Chesapeake Bay, is St. Michael's Manor. The land of the original estate was one of three manors south of Smith Creek granted to Governor Leonard Calvert in 1639, "with the right of Court Baron and Court Leet."

St. Michael's Manor probably was built by James L. Richardson about 1805. There is a brick in the house, formerly in a cornerstone, that says, J.L.R., 1805. Other families who have owned the house are the Langleys, the Milburns, the Williamson Smiths, and the Visek's. In 1982 it was purchased by the present owners, Capt. and Mrs. Joseph L. Dick. The Richardson family are all buried in a graveyard in the woods, some 150 yards north of the manor, enclosed with a wrought-iron fence. James Richardson died in 1824.

The two-and-a-half storey house lies within fifty feet of the water in a meadow almost level with the cove. It faces the road now, but at one time the front door opened on the water side. From the wide brick ends rise chimneys which are flush with the walls. A small entrance porch is on the road side. To the right is a small one storey wing and a slave cabin, in line with the house.

The entrance leads to a hall running through the house to the back door. The front door is quite interesting as it has flush panelling on the outside and sunken on the inner side. Both doors have old locks which were made and patented in England by J. Young. In the two small low-ceilinged rooms on the first floor there is no panelling, but a chair rail runs around the walls. As the ground-water level is near the surface there is no cellar.

The original small twisted stairway was re-done in the 1960's and is now wider. There is no panelling on the first floor stairway, but there is on the second and third floors. It is rather remarkable that the second storey should have the benefit of the panelling instead of the first. Perhaps the family had their living quarters on this floor and conducted business matters below. There is an attic which is lighted by dormer windows. Many of the doors in St. Michael's Manor are hung from the original H and HL hinges.

Tradition has it that the bricks in this house came from England, and it is said that one can see the remains of the boat which carried them, sunk in the cove. Aunt Mary Pidgeon, an aged negress living near the Manor and reputed to be one hundred and fifteen years old, quotes her grandmother as supporting this story. However, the bricks themselves seem to have the same characteristics as those found in other houses of the same period in St. Mary's County.

SOTTERLEY

Sotterley Road, Hollywood

If the "Rose of Sotterley" were to come back to the home in St. Mary's County in which she lived one hundred and eighty years ago, she would find little change. Restored to the condition in which it was in 1776, after many years of research by the late Herbert Satterlee and Mrs. Mabel Satterlee Ingalls, president of Sotterley Mansion Foundations, Inc., the house still looks out over the calm waters of the Patuxent River just opposite St. Leonard's Creek. The view from the hill on which Sotterley is situated is superb, and the gardens are just as they were laid out when the house was built.

It was before 1689 that the first George Plater came to Maryland and married Ann Burford. Their son, George, married the Widow Bowles, June 10, 1728, and on "Bowles Separation", a part of "Resurrection Manor" which she brought him as a dowry, built a house in 1730. The new residence was named by him in honor of Sotterley in Suffolk, England, the ancestral home of his family, the Sotterleys.

The house, which faces the East, consists of the main building one hundred and two feet long, with a library wing at right angles and detached kitchen. It is of brick and timber, with cellar and foundations of salmon brick. All the brass, hardware, glass, and stone porch pavement came from England. The ivy-covered gable-ends are of brick and so are the floors of the rear porches. There are dormer windows on a rather steep roof which is capped by a small cupola. There are two brick garden houses, two gate lodges, a spinning house, custom house, and brick warehouse which bears the date 1757.

Sotterley's interior is noted for its Great Hall, which has been cited as one of the one hundred most beautiful rooms in America. The main hall, library, wing room, and study are panelled in local pine painted white. Carved shell motifs adorn the quaint alcoves flanking the fireplace. The master carpentry was all done by an indentured servant, Richard Boulton, around 1750. He also designed and built the remarkable Chinese Chippendale mahogany stairs and gallery on the second floor. This boasts a grooved hand rail and a wonderfully wrought newel post.

Sotterley breathes romance and mystery. Some say that the muffled oarlocks of the funeral barge of Governor Plater, son of the builder, can be heard on the river on still nights. Mistress Ann Rousby Plater, reputed to be one of the most beautiful women of Maryland, lived and died there, and after her, "The Rose of Sotterley," daughter-in-law of the governor. Ghostly figures took part in early morning duels. Long sessions at cards and gay parties enlivened the countryside. In fact, George Plater, the Governor's grandson, lost Sotterley at dice to Colonel Somerville of Mulberry Fields. The latter wasted little time in selling the property to Colonel Thomas Barber. His two daughters were the heirs, and the one who received the mansion and four hundred and seventy-five acres of land, married Dr. W.H.S. Briscoe. He made several changes in the architectural arrangements including the closing of a secret passage which led from the cellar to some point on the grounds. Herbert Satterlee restored the mansion to its original form after he bought the property in 1910. The plantation now includes fifteen hundred and fifty-six acres.

Sotterley Mansion is open to the public daily from June 1 to September 30, 11:00 A.M. to 5:00 P.M. and may also be visited in April, May, October, and November by appointment.

SUSQUEHANNA

Patuxent River

In St. Mary's County on a bluff high above the Patuxent River, which meets the Chesapeake Bay here, and two miles from Jarboesville, there used to stand a long, low, and rather sinister-looking house known as Susquehanna. Its early history bears out its appearance, for it was while Christopher Rousby, the King's Collector-General, was living here that he "was taken out of this world by a violent death, received on Board His Majesty's Ship, the *Quaker Ketch.*" The tragedy occurred in an argument with Colonel George Talbot, Surgeon-General of the Province. Talbot was arrested and taken to Virginia, but managed to escape and ultimately won his freedom. In the same tomb with his brother lies John Rousby, who died three months later on February 1, 1685, just as he was about to land in Maryland. This tomb, plainly marked with a large marble slab, lies in a field about two hundred yards from the site of the house.

Susquehanna was standing before 1661, as the Colonial Council held its meeting there on July 1, when it was decided to undertake an expedition against the Dutch on the Delaware. It was probably built some years before this, about 1650.

The house was erected in two sections, the first being the northern end, with its semi-detached outside chimney. This small cabin later was enlarged until it reached its present length of sixty feet. Susquehanna is only fifteen feet wide, but the two porches front and back make it seem larger. The building is of frame construction, the irregular pattern of its clapboards showing their handmade origin.

This house is one of the few early homes built to be approached from the land side. The dormer windows and the position of the stairs both point to this assumption.

The rooms and their lack of decoration indicate the early date at which the house was erected. The staircases are small and strictly utilitarian. There is no touch of the elegance which characterizes Cross Manor, built ten years earlier. The rooms are small, especially on the second floor, where there are four dormer windows. There are no dormer windows on the side that formerly overlooked the bay. This very dearth of ornamentation is rather charming, although no decoration could remove the faint air of mystery which hovers over Susquehanna.

In support of this feeling a trap door in the wooden front porch led to a small cellar, five feet square and seven feet deep, which was probably used as a wine cellar. However, fearsome stories are told of pirates hiding the bodies of their victims there until they could be removed and flung into the bay.

At the death of John Rousby in 1684, the property reverted to the Proprietary, and in 1700 it was granted to Richard Smith. It came into the Carroll family when Captain Henry Carroll married the niece of Colonel John Rousby. Susquehanna remained in possession of the Carrolls until 1881, when Colonel Henry James died. The property was acquired from Samuel David Young, of Grand Rapids, Michigan, by the Department of the Navy in 1940 for construction of the Patuxent River Naval Air Station. Through Mr. Young's acquaintance with Henry Ford, Susquehanna House was dismantled and moved to the Greenfield Village, Dearborn, Michigan, where it can still be seen.

TUDOR HALL

Tudor Hall Road, Leonardtown

Near the river in Leonardtown, with an entrance branching off from the main road, is Tudor Hall, known far and wide as the ancestral home of the Key family. However, contrary to popular belief, Francis Scott Key never visited here.

This Colonial dwelling was built about 1760 by Abraham Barnes. When he died in 1800 he specified that his three hundred slaves be freed on condition that they take his name, which explains why there are so many blacks of that name in Maryland. Mr. Mason of Virginia, the next owner, sold the house to Philip Key. In 1949 it was purchased by Mary Patterson Davidson and donated to the citizens of St. Mary's County for use as a public library. In January 1984, the public library will be moving to a new location and Tudor Hall will revert to the Davidson heirs.

Tudor Hall is two-and-a-half storeys high. From the evidence of the timbers and the constructions of the ends of the building it would seem that the house originally had a shape similar to that of Batchelor's Hope, in the same section of Maryland. Henry Chandlee Forman also advances this theory in his book, "Early Manor and Plantation Houses of Maryland."

The most striking feature of the building is the inset portico. This has four large pillars of white plastered brick and is set in five feet.

A few steps lead up to the charming leaded door which opens into the hall. A staircase, on the right, rising in a sweeping curve immediately before the entrance, is well conceived and beautifully executed. The large and well lighted rooms on the ground floor have fireplaces with simple mantels.

A central medallion of plaster adorns the ceilings of the central hall. The kitchen is a replica constructed after 1920. It has served as the library's children's room for the past 13 years. The house has a large cellar, entrance to which is gained by an arched brick opening.

In the rear of Tudor Hall a lofty yew tree towers over the roof. It is one of the oldest of its kind in Maryland. The grounds slope down to the river, distant a few hundred yards. To the right of the Hall and about a quarter of a mile away is the private graveyard of the Barnes family.

Legend has it that on moonlit nights the ghost of Joseph Key is accustomed to take his ease on the porch in a rocking chair. Should one not be available, Mr. Key marches into the house and gets himself a rocker which he takes to the porch and sets down with a vindictive bang. Then he slowly seats himself and rocks serenely to and fro in the beauty of the night.

PARROTT'S CAGE

Cage Road, St. Leonard

On the banks of the placid Patuxent River, about a quarter of a mile from the water, stands a small one-and-a-half storey dwelling with dormer windows. It has been known as Parrott's Cage ever since its original owner, William Parrott, settled there in 1650. The dwelling itself was not finished until 1652, which makes it one of the oldest buildings in Maryland. This two room brick house is one of the few which have been in the same family from the time the grant was first made. William Parrott married Ann MacKall, and their daughter, who inherited the property, married Dr. Thomas Parran. The dwelling has been in the Parran family since, and is now occupied by Benjamin Parran III. One of the owners was Dr. Thomas Parran, a famous surgeon during the American Revolution and a founder of St. John's College.

The walls of the facades have been painted white, but it can still be seen that they were constructed of Flemish bond brick with glazed headers. Over the windows are serpentine arches of an unusual type. A plain wooden moulding runs under the eaves.

A small porch shades the front door which opens directly into the sitting room or parlor. A door in line with the front door would seem to substantiate the idea that there was a partition (removed by a later owner) making a hall from front to back. A large fireplace projects into the room. In the left hand corner there was a winding staircase which led to the second floor, but it has been gone for decades.

Some years ago the great great grandfather of the present owner had all the panelling ripped out of the house and chopped up for firewood. Benjamin Parran, Sr., had it carefully restored by one of the few men in Maryland who was able to execute this type of craftsmanship. Of the two rooms, the left has the northern end panelled to the ceiling, with two inset cupboards. A wainscoting three feet high encircles the other walls, as much like the old panelling as was possible.

The second room has a modern fireplace and contains a very pleasing feature in a wooden ceiling and uncovered aged beams. The windows in this room, as well as those in the parlor, are fairly small and deep set. About ninety years ago a wing was added, where the kitchen is now located.

Additions were completed in the 1940's and 1950's, making Parrott's Cage a large house. It is the main dwelling for one of, if not the largest farms in Calvert County. It may well have been the last glimpse of the plantation system, as there are several frame buildings that were built for tenant farmers, but now standing empty.

This section of Calvert County is rich in history and legend. Not far away, down the river, is Preston-on-Patuxent, sometime capitol of the Province of Maryland. Eltonhead and his Cavalier army must have been in the neighborhood when they tried to depose the Colonial followers of Cromwell. There also are old wives' tales that pirates sailed the Patuxent, although there is no record saying that they molested the Parrans of Parrott's Cage.

PRESTON-ON-PATUXENT

Turner Road, Lusby

At the end of a long lane two miles from Lusby, facing the Patuxent River, lies Preston-on-Patuxent, erected in 1650. The land was patented in 1652 by Richard Preston, called "the Great Quaker" by Governor Charles Calvert. He was also a Commissioner of Maryland under Oliver Cromwell, the Lord Protector. His grandson, the last of his name, was Mayor of Philadelphia.

The house itself is much like the neighboring Parrott's Cage. One-and-a-half storeys high with three dormer windows, this home is larger than most of the dwellings built in the early days of the Colony. Alternating blue glazed and red bricks run up to a wooden moulding under the eaves. There are small brick chimneys at either end of the rectangular house, which is capped with a peaked roof of hand-rived shingles. The present owners have made extensive and pleasant alterations. The modern wing, forming a courtyard in the rear, is so much in keeping with the period that at first sight it is impossible to distinguish it from the original mansion.

Upon entering Preston-on-Patuxent from a small brick landing, one steps immediately into a huge room occupying the whole of the lower floor of the original building. A partition put in during the eighteenth century has been removed. At either end of the room enormous fireplaces of brick jut out into the room. The chimney pieces recede toward the ceiling. These fireplaces are remarkable in that they have a round arch instead of the usual square opening, and are about seven feet wide and correspondingly deep.

From floor to ceiling the whole of this charming room is covered with panelling of Maryland pine, ten feet nine inches high, making the room look even larger than it is. The rectangles in the panelling are large and made of a single board planed and fitted by hand. One section of this has small dentils under the ceiling moulding, showing where the partition was removed. The windows are deeply recessed and larger than is usual in houses of this early Colonial period. On the right of the fireplace in the northern end of the house are winding steps, not used at present, leading to the second floor.

At one time the important men of the Colony gathered at this small house, as it was the capitol of Maryland from 1654 to 1659. All the records from St. Mary's City were brought here after the fall of Governor Stone.

Owned by the Gantts for several generations, the property was bought in by John Breeden at a tax sale. The next owner was Hulbert Footner, the well known novelist, whose wife was the daughter of Dr. William H. Marsh of Solomon's. When they purchased the old home in 1912, Mr. and Mrs. Footner changed the name of Preston-at-Patuxent to that of Charles' Gift, another grant which belonged to Richard Preston.

The present owners are Dr. and Mrs. John H. Cumberland who have extensively restored the house and also restored its original name, Preston-on-Patuxent. The Cumberlands gave an historic easement to the Maryland Historical Trust, which conducted an archeological survey of an Indian village on the property in 1983.

ROUSBY HALL

Rousby Hall Road, Lusby

One of southern Maryland's most historic properties, Rousby Hall has been beautifully restored to its late 17th century appearance. Once a series of plantations totalling 5,000 acres, Rousby Hall was the estate of three John Rousbys who were King Charles I's men in Maryland. The Rousby clan was in constant conflict with Lord Baltimore and their actions were supported by the British monarch who once put Lord Baltimore on probation at John Rousby's plea.

The Rousby family owned both sides of Maryland's longest river, the Patuxent, the tracts then being in Calvert County. Drum Point, the Ranch Club development and hundreds of homes along the area's many creeks all once were part of Rousby Hall, now 20.89 acres with 800 feet of sandy beach and 1,100 feet on Rousby Hall Road.

The first John Rousby probably resided in the existing Rousby Hall while awaiting the building of a brick mansion destined to be bombed by the British in the Revolutionary War because it was thought to harbor Joshua Barney, leader of the American gunboat flotilla that harassed British naval forces. Rebuilt, the manor house was bombed again in 1814 as British forces went up the Patuxent enroute to burning Washington.

Christopher Rousby, brother of the first John Rousby, was stabbed to death in 1685 aboard the ship Baltimore anchored at the mouth of the Patuxent by Col. George Talbot, cousin of Lord Baltimore, who had served as Deputy Governor of Maryland. Talbot was imprisoned aboard ship, then in a Virginia jail awaiting hanging, when he was set free by his wife and a band of servants. He was recaptured, but King Charles, responding to Lord Baltimore's plea, allowed Talbot to return to England.

John Rousby inherited his brother's estate on what is now the vast 6800 acre Patuxent Naval Air Station in St. Mary's County. But John Rousby shortly died of natural causes and his son John II for a time held both properties. Christopher Rousby's home, known as Susquehanna, and the present Rousby Hall are exact duplicates built before 1800.

Owned by newspaper publisher-editor Elmer M. Jackson, Jr. (a retired Navy Commander) and his wife Doris Grace Jackson, Rousby Hall has been restored by them to its original beauty based on records, art work and pictures gathered from former owners. Rousby Hall and its cottage are furnished with antiques from the Jacksons' antique shop in Annapolis. The cottage built around 1682 by order of King Charles was Maryland's first customs house. All ships coming to Maryland docked here to declare their cargo and pay fees to the king. This ancient cottage is a small gem, our State's first treasury building. In 1983 much of the waterfront of Rousby was bulkheaded for the first time with the cooperation of the Maryland Department of Natural Resources.

Rousby Hall has a huge living room with a high ceiling and huge, tall windows. The equally spacious dining room is ideal for entertaining especially in the summer when the huge front porch can also be used. A large kitchen, a study, and the enclosed porch are among the facilities of the main floor. Three large bedrooms constitute the second floor. Every room has its own working fireplace.

One of the show places in the 11 acre lawn area is the grave of John Rousby III who died at age 23 in 1750. His brick tomb with a marble slab contains the Rousby coat of arms. Anne, widow of John Rousby III, was known as the White Rose of Maryland and also being wealthy she was besieged with suitors. She bore John Rousby a daughter Elizabeth who married Maryland Governor George Plater and one time she also owned Sotterley estate, now restored and open to tourists.

Gorgeous Anne Rousby wed widower William Fitzhugh of Virginia out of fear after rejecting his suit seven times. The persistent but dejected Fitzhugh was leaving Rousby Hall to return to his boat when he spied a nurse carrying baby Elizabeth. Grabbing the child he ran to his boat and ordered his men to shove off. Anne at the beach frantically pled for the baby's safe return but Fitzhugh said he would drown the baby unless Anne married him. Anne surrendered to his demands, and they had a happy and fruitful marriage.

HABRE DE VENTURE

Rose Hill Road, Port Tobacco

About three miles west of La Plata, on the west side of Rose Hill Road, stands Habre de Venture, built in 1771 by Thomas Stone, a signer of the Declaration of Independence. Stone was born in Charles County, but moved to Annapolis in his early years to study law under Thomas Johnson. In 1764, he was admitted to the Maryland Bar, and moved to Frederick.

Thomas Stone chose a Charles County bride, Margaret Brown, daughter of Dr. Gustavus Richard Brown, a physician to George Washington. After the death of his father, Daniel Stone, Thomas, along with his mother Elizabeth Jenifer Stone, and his younger brother, John Hoskins Stone, who later became Governor of Maryland, returned to his native county. Though at first Thomas was a loyal British subject, defending the poll tax in court, in 1775, as a delegate to the Continental Congress, he signed the petition of protest, and the following year, abandoning any hope for reconciliation, the Declaration of Independence.

Thomas Stone continued to serve his state and country as State Senator and as a delegate to Congress under the Articles of Confederation. In 1787, he was chosen as a delegate to the Constitutional Convention, a position he declined due to failing health. He died on October 5 of that year. From that time until 1945, Habre de Venture remained in the hands of Thomas Stone's descendants.

In 1945, Peter Vischer, a New York newspaper and magazine publisher, and his wife, an author known by her maiden name Helen Lombard, purchased Habre de Venture, restored the house, and established a stable in which to breed thoroughbred horses. Even after Mr. Vischer's death in 1970, Mrs. Vischer continued to hold a Maryland racing license. On New Year's Day of 1977, the house was ravaged by fire, destroying the central section and severely damaging the kitchen wing. The east wing, which was Thomas Stone's law office, survived intact.

During the following three years, the house and 321 acres have been acquired by the National Park Service, which will restore the house and operate the area as the Thomas Stone National Historic Site. Its purposes are to commemorate the life and career of Thomas Stone in the light of the war for independence and the development of a new nation, and to provide an understanding of 18th century life as Thomas Stone lived it.

The house itself is architecturally important, being an irregular five-part manor-style house composed of three different early building methods and arranged in an arc. The central section is a brick, one and one-half storey house with a gambrel roof. Both the north and south elevations are composed of five bays each, one of which in both cases is a door.

The hyphen to the northwest is a section of the house in its own right, but smaller, with an elevated gambrel roof. This brick section is three bays long, with two dormers. To the east of the central section is a small, one and one-half storey gambrel roof structure with no dormers and constructed of frame.

The most famous interior feature was the panelling in the living room. Fortunately, this original panelling was sold to the Baltimore Museum of Art by Michael Stone, one of the 20th century owners, and so it escaped the fire.

HARD BARGAIN

West Hatton Road, Mount Victoria

This telescopic masterpiece is built on a hill in Charles County, and its shape, peculiar but not unusual in Southern Maryland, can be seen from the Wicomico River. The gables and the chimneys print a gaunt silhouette against the sky. The house is in three sections which total eighty feet in length, and is built entirely of brick. There was an air of neglect about Hard Bargain, as the trees and shrubs that had surrounded it once are almost all gone, with the exception of a ruined square box-wood garden lying to the south of the house. When it was purchased in the 1930s by Mr. and Mrs. Franklin F. Olmsted of New York, they planned to landscape the grounds as well as to redecorate the interior. Their son, Franklin B. Olmsted, an attorney in La Plata, is the current owner.

The plain exterior, broken by many windows, is ornamented by a brick corbel cornice and a rather fine square transom over the main doorway, which do little to relieve the stern effect of the house. It is a well built and sturdy example of the step construction of which the early Colonials were so fond. The northwest side of the dwelling is laid in Flemish bond.

Erected about the year 1768, there are two vastly different stories on how it came to be. The first and more likely story, is that the land was bought by Gwynn Harris, owner of nearby Mt. Tirzah, for his brother, Tom. It seems that Tom didn't get along with Gwynn's wife, Kitty Root Harris. Gwynn promised to buy him a farm and build him a house if Tom would make up with Kitty and kiss her, which Tom promptly did. Gwynn, although he had to be reminded the next day, was true to his word, purchased the land and put up the house, where Tom lived to a ripe old age. Although Gwynn called it a Hard Bargain, some say it was Tom who thought the bargain hard.

A second story was that John Maddox, a gambler for high stakes, bought the land and had a house constructed for which he paid in full. Shortly afterwards he had the bad luck to lose his newly built home in a card game, and had to buy it back from his more fortunate opponent. Maddox was then heard to remark, with pardonable bitterness, that it was a hard bargain to pay twice for the same house.

The plan of the dwelling is such that one enters at the southern end where there is a fine stairway with beautifully carved step-ends, leading to the second storey. Also in excellent taste is the decoration of the mantels, and they, as well as the careful brick work and large gracefully proportioned rooms throughout the house, show that the builder did not stint his materials. The cellar runs only under the main section of the building.

Hard Bargain was originally a part of Wicomico Fields, but John Maddox separated the land from its original grant. After Tom Harris' death, it was purchased by the Digges family and known as Digges' Farm. In 1861, John Mitchell, trustee, conveyed the land to Susan R. Morton. Mort S. Laurence sold the property to the late Robert Crain in 1904, from whose estate it was bought in 1930 by the Maryland Realty Investment Trust. The once proud residence of the Harris' and the Digges' was then purchased by the Olmsteds.

MOUNT REPUBLICAN

Old Crain Highway, Newburg

Stately Mount Republican rears its ivy clad walls on a hill in Charles County a mile from the juncture of the Potomac and Wicomico rivers. Its beautiful brick work, tall double chimneys, and smooth gable-ends blend into a perfect artistic and architectural picture. The wooden cornice is decorated with guttae, chains, metopes of diamonds, and triglyphs of flutes. The southern end has a diamond pattern in glazed brick; the northern end a bull's-eye window high in the bricks.

English boxwood and magnolia trees line the drive, which is directly in line with the main entrance and leads from the Crain Highway a few hundred yards away. A garden with a frog pond and blossoming trees lies behind the house, surrounded by its acres of wide fields and heavily wooded hills, sloping to the broad Potomac. There are also a swimming pool and bath house next to the gardens.

Mount Republican is a worthy example of the best type of eighteenth century American architecture. One of the best specimens of fanlight doorways in Maryland leads into the entrance hall that runs through the mansion to a duplicate door in the rear. From the entrance hall to the second storey and attic rises a broad walnut stairway. The rooms are square, with lofty ceilings, tall windows, and large fireplaces. On the first floor are the sitting room and dining room, entered from the hall. A new addition houses the servants' quarters and the kitchen. The former kitchen is now used as a clubroom. The second floor is arranged with a room over each of those on the lower floor, with an extra room over the hall. The attic is large and from it a trap door leads to the roof. From this vantage point there is a magnificent view. A most in-teresting feature is the pond in the shape of a heart, which was constructed as a Valentine's gift.

Harry Yates, who built the house in 1792, swore that he would live under his own roof and had the attic finished first. Nonetheless, he never stayed there as he was killed by a kick from his horse at Mrs. George Dent's before the building was completed. Theophilus Yates, said to be of royal descent, was the next owner and at his death the estate passed to his two children, Robert and Jane. Robert died and his sister inherited the whole property, which was her dowry when she married Francis Hawkins. Franklin Weems lived in the house in the eighteenth century. He was known as the King Entertainer of Southern Maryland because of his lavish hospitality. The story of a forty year poker game, which is reputed to have taken place there, is a bit doubtful. Records tell that Mary H. Hawkins sold Mount Republican to Henry H. Richmond in 1888, who, in turn, sold it to Robert Crain. At his death the house and land were purchased from his estate by the Maryland Realty Investment Trust which sold the house to R. Kennedy Hanson of Pittsburgh. Mr. Hanson sold the house to Mr. F. Bowie Addison, from whom it was purchased in 1973 by the present owners, Mrs. and Mrs. Gordon O'Neill.

The genial ghosts of lusty men and beautiful women seem to be ever present in the rooms of the Georgian mansion, for few houses in Maryland have such an atmosphere of welcome and old-fashioned friendliness. One of the most charming sights is watching the lights coming on at sunset across the Potomac in Virginia.

SOCIETY HILL

Mount Victoria Road, Mount Victoria

In 1664 Captain Humphrey Warren, a London merchant, descended from William the Conqueror, Queen Mathilda of Flanders, Emperor Charlemagne and Alfred the Great, received a Proprietary grant of 300 acres called Frailty on the western shore of the Wicomico River in what is now Charles County, Md.

The property passed down through Capt. Warren's family until 1784 when Thomas Hungerford purchased 244 acres and the house now known as Society Hill. At his death in 1798 it passed down through the Hungerford family until it was sold to Dr. Andrew J. Smoot in 1887. Justus H. Ehlers purchased it from the Smoot heirs in 1907. He sold to Robert Crain in 1913. In 1937 Mary Moore Warner purchased it from Wallastons Manor Corp., making some renovations at that time.

Society Hill is located near Mt. Victoria and situated on a high ridge with a commanding view of the Wicomico River. The house appears to have been built circa 1700-1730. It was constructed of brick nogging with beaded wood siding covering the nogging. It has a full cellar with two pents, a dirt floor and wood grilles in the four cellar windows. There are porches on each side of the house and free-standing chimneys on each end. In one of the chimneys are two doorways, one with a flat and one with an arched top, the sole example of this architecture in Maryland. The smaller chimney is fitted with shelves and the larger with a small niche. These doors led into a wing destroyed in the early 20th century. A modern kitchen was built in its place. An enclosed passage originally extended from this room to the old kitchen to the east. The old kitchen was of wood, with a large brick fireplace, containing one room at ground level and one room above, with a ladder being used for access to the upper room which had a small window at each end.

An unusual feature is that the "family" room projects onto the front porch. That porch has two doors. The door on the left leads into an office, the other into the main hall which runs through to the other porch overlooking the river.

On the left as you enter the hallway is a staircase enclosed in its own well, winding about a central post to the second floor. Further down the hall to the left is the living room. On the right, as you enter the hall, is the room presently designated "family" room, then almost directly opposite the living room door is the door to the dining room.

The present property consists of 355 acres and was sold by Mrs. Warner in 1962 to the present owners, Mr. & Mrs. Charles E. Wegner.

WEST HATTON

West Hatton Road, Mount Victoria

In Charles County on the shores of the Wicomico River, almost directly across from Chaptico Bay, and two and a half miles from Mount Victoria Post Office, is West Hatton. The property was granted to Thomas Hatton, the bearer to Maryland of the Act of Religious Toleration. While the old estate is still known as West Hatton, it had been in the Stoddert family for so many generations that the water front on which it is located is now referred to on all maps as Stoddert's Point. West Hatton now comprises a land area of approximately seven hundred acres, with two and a half miles of gravel shore on the Wicomico River.

West Hatton was not the first home erected on the property. Crumbling foundations of others were there in 1784, when Major William Truman Stoddert, a nephew and member of the staff of the Revolutionary War hero, General Smallwood, selected this point almost encircled by the river on which to build. The property, which has been in the Stoddert family ever since, was inherited by Major Truman Stoddert, son of William Truman and Elizabeth Gwinn Stoddert. Major John Truman Stoddert's grandson, William Truman Stoddert, inherited from him; and his daughter, Elizabeth, who married Foster M. Reeder, came into the estate upon the death of her grandmother. West Hatton is currently owned by the von Busshe family from Germany.

West Hatton stands at the end of a long lane behind a white picket fence, the gateway of which frames the front door. Flanked on the left by a one storey wing and on the right by a two storey structure, the central section flaunts great square double chimneys cutting through the roof at either end. On the east there is a small entrance porch shading the front door, while the river side has a two storey porch running the full length of the main section. The first storey of the porch is upheld by large round brick pillars tapering toward the top and covered with white plaster. Many years ago, while being reconditioned, the entire house was covered with stucco, but this was removed in 1934, revealing the old bricks in excellent condition.

As one enters the Colonial door with its leaded tracery fanlight and side-lights, the steps appear on the right of the hall immediately behind the door to the drawing room. The walnut stairs lead up to the attic in graceful flights, so well built that there has been no sag since this main portion of the house was erected about 1794. On the left of the hall is a door and a short flight of steps leading down into the library, which has fine corner cupboards flanking the mantel. At the end of the hall is the door to the paved brick porch and the garden.

The dining room opens off the drawing room and in both rooms fireplaces of similar style are found with oval medallions in the panels and narrow eared shelves. In between the two rooms is a fine example of a panelled double door with an arched fanlight of leaded tracery above it. In the garden are the graves of many generations of Stodderts which have been marked by one plain stone, placed there by Elizabeth Stoddert Reeder.

BELAIR

12207 Tulip Grove Drive, Bowie

For many years, Belair was the property of the Ogle family and became known as "the home of Governors." The history of Belair began with the land on which it stands. In 1683 a 500-acre tract called "Catton" was patented to Robert Carvile of St. Mary's City. In 1698 Carvile conveyed the tract to Colonel Henry Ridgley. In 1721 the Reverend Jacob Henderson, then owner, changed the name to "Belair." In March 1737 Henderson sold the estate to Governor Samuel Ogle and Benjamin Tasker, Sr. In August of that year Ogle became the sole owner.

Ogle served three non-consecutive terms as Governor of the Province. Samuel Ogle, in July 1741, married Anne Tasker, daughter of his former partner. In the latter part of 1742 they went to England. During the four years they were abroad, her father was in charge of building the original central portion of the mansion. They returned in 1747 and almost immediately built a detached 40-foot brick, two storey kitchen-office east of the house.

Built of brick, it is two storeys in height above a moderately high basement, seven bays in length, with a low-pitched gambrel roof. Both long facades contain a center door with an equal number of windows on either side. On these long facades and the two ends of the 18th century section, the bricks are laid in English bond while the bond of the fourth (south) side is Flemish with glazed headers presenting a checkered effect. The entrance is through the north but the south facade, facing the spectacular view over the broad terraces, is treated architecturally as the more important with the projecting pavilion three bays in width. About five feet above the ground there is a beveled water table and at the second floor level is a belt course which extends all around the center block, four courses in height.

Samuel Ogle died in May 1752 leaving Benjamin Tasker, Sr. and Benjamin Tasker, Jr. as executors of his Will and guardians of his young son, Benjamin Ogle. Benjamin Tasker, Jr. carried out a number of improvements. Still standing are the rows of tulip poplar trees he planted to the north of the house. On the downspout at the building's west end are the initials "B.T." and the date 1757, the year of its installation.

Benjamin Tasker, Jr. died in 1760 and his father ran Belair until his death in 1768. When young Benjamin Ogle attained his majority in 1770 he gained possession of Belair. It was he who established the deer park at Belair and from its fine English stock sent six fawns to George Washington at Mount Vernon.

Benjamin Ogle served three one-year terms as State Governor, beginning in 1798. Prior to that time he had deeded Belair to his son, Benjamin Ogle II. Much of the present interior of the central portion was installed by him around 1810. Benjamin Ogle II and his wife, Anna Maria, raised their 14 children at Belair. Difficult times in the mid-1800s and the aftermath of the Civil War forced the Ogles to place mortgages on the estate. They were unable to meet these obligations and the property was sold by court order. From 1871 until 1898 a series of families owned Belair for short periods of time.

In 1898 the estate was purchased by James T. Woodward. He made several improvements and added the hyphen and wing to the west end. On his death in 1910, he bequeathed Belair to his nephew, William Woodward, Sr., who built the hyphen and wing on the east. The Woodward era came to an end with the tragic death in 1955 of William Woodward, Jr.

Two years later the Levitt Corporation purchased the estate and for a time used the mansion as an office. In 1964 Levitt sold the building and about five and a half acres surrounding it to the City of Bowie. Until 1977 it functioned as City Hall.

Belair Mansion was added to the National Register of Historic Places on November 11, 1977. It is open to the public on the second Sunday of every month (2-4:00 p.m.) and each Wednesday (10:00 a.m. until 1:00 p.m.). Special tours may be arranged through Bowie City Hall.

DUMBLANE

Westphalia Road, Upper Marlboro

Prince George's County is renowned for its great mansions in the pure Georgian style. But there are a number of less pretentious dwellings such as Wyoming, the Marbury home, built about 1759; Sasscer's Green; and Want Water, patented in 1708 by Colonel Thomas Addison, Lord Baltimore's Privy Councelor. Dumblane was another house in this category.

Hidden by shrubbery along the narrow road, Dumblane emerged quite suddenly in all its quaint charm as though it had been designed for that one spot. It stood about three miles from Forestville in a district of rolling hills, wooded slopes, and fertile meadows. Although there was no river view, the vista was as beautiful in its way as is that which is to be seen from Mt. Airy in St. Mary's County.

Dumblane was erected in 1723 by John Magruder, the son of Alexander Magruder. It remained in the family for generations, finally coming into the possession of Miss Eleanor Magruder. The next owner was Francis M. Bowie, her nephew, who made it his country home until his death in 1877. Dumblane was destroyed in 1969.

The house had three sides of brick, which were later covered in stucco. It measured only forty feet long and thirty-one feet wide. The east facade, constructed of frame covered with clapboard, was five bays long. The long catslide roof without dormers, in the rear, was one of the interesting features. On the north and south gables were two chimneys with many diagonal recesses, partially projecting from the walls. These are rare in Maryland, but there are other examples, among them those at Bellefield and Marlboro House.

Outside of the living room door were the stairs which crossed the end of the hall above a cupboard. On the left of the hall stood the door to the parlor which was smaller than the living room. Another fireplace had been in line with the parlor door.

A large closet was built between the chimneys on the south side of the house. In the rear of the parlor was the narrow dining room with a small fireplace, a corner cupboard, and a little trap door in the ceiling leading into the attic. The kitchen opened off the dining room. A small bedroom was entered either from the dining room or the living room. The rooms upstairs were all small with sloping roofs. The fenestration was quite irregular, some windows being so small that they might have been designed originally as loopholes.

The graveyard of the Magruders is near the site of the house. The weathered eighteenth century headstones testify to the family's long residence at Dumblane.

The quaint roof line and staggered chimneys brought vividly to mind the Scotch cottages which the builders had left behind in their native country. Maryland was singularly fortunate in having so many home-loving men from across the sea who clung to their native architecture rather than being content with any crude roof that would keep out the weather.

MONTPELIER

Route 197, Laurel

Southeast of Laurel, just off Maryland Route 197, stands Montpelier, one of the finest houses in Prince George's County. Set on the crest of a gentle slope, it enjoys a beautiful view of rolling countryside.

The mansion was built by Major Thomas and Ann Ridgely Snowden, and as a result of recent research, the time of its construction has been placed at 1780-1783. Major Snowden was a descendant of Richard Snowden, a Welshman, who had come to Maryland in the 17th century. Through several generations the family had accumulated vast landholdings which extended into parts of Prince George's, Anne Arundel, Montgomery and Howard counties. On a portion of "Snowden's New Birmingham Manor" which he inherited from his father, Major Snowden built his home.

In appearance it is similar to the Hammond-Harwood House in Annapolis. It is all of brick with a central two-story block flanked on both sides by lower hyphens which connect it with wings at each end. The effect against the sky, however, is quite different. In contrast to the low roof line of the Annapolis house, Montpelier's roof is high and, because of its steep pitch, all of its lines seem to converge toward a single point.

On the death of Major Thomas in 1803, his son Nicholas inherited the house. Nicholas and his sizeable family occupied it until he died in 1831. At that time it passed into the possession of his daughter Julianna and her husband, Dr. Theodore Jenkins. The last Snowdens to own Montpelier were three of Julianna's children, Arthur, Elizabeth

and Mary Jenkins, who sold it in 1888. Through the following decades Montpelier passed through several owners including Edmund H. Pendleton, an author of some reputation, and Emmanuel Havenith, Minister-plenipetentiary from Belgium.

In 1928 the estate was purchased by Mr. and Mrs. Breckinridge Long. Long served as United States Ambassador to Italy from 1933 to 1936 and was a presidential appointee to the State Department during the administrations of Woodrow Wilson and Franklin D. Roosevelt. After the deaths of the Longs in the late 1950's, the property was acquired by the Maryland-National Capital Park and Planning Commission.

Montpelier's walls have sheltered any number of distinguished guests. Washington stayed there twice in 1787 on his way to and from the Constitutional Convention. In 1789, as they traveled to New York for the inauguration of the first president, Martha Washington and her party spent a night. And Abigail Adams enjoyed the hospitality of the Snowdens as she moved southward to join her husband in Washington. During the Longs' ownership many of the leading personages of the Roosevelt era attended social functions at the lovely country home.

While Montpelier's official address is 9401 Montpelier Drive, Laurel 20708, access to the mansion's grounds is via Muirkirk Road. Many special events are held each year at Montpelier, and the house is open to the public for tours at certain times. For specific information, contact the History Division, Maryland-National Capital Park and Planning Commission, at (301) 779-2011.

MOUNT AIRY

Rosaryville Road, Upper Marlboro

Not far from the hamlet of Rosaryville on a winding road, quietly nestling in its extensive grounds, is Mount Airy, reputed to have been built about 1660 as a hunting lodge by Charles Calvert. The land was patented in 1705 as Darnall's Lodge by Colonel Henry Darnall, brother-in-law of the Third Lord Baltimore and resident of nearby Woodyard.

Subsequently, the property was passed through several actions to Samuel Hyde of London, who conveyed it as payment of a debt to Charles Calvert, the Fifth Lord Baltimore, in 1745. In 1749, it was deeded to his son, Benedict Calvert, and the house was burned down in 1752. It was promptly rebuilt, as Benedict lived there from 1752 until his death in 1788, followed in unbroken lineage by his descendants until 1902. George Washington visited Mount Airy in 1774 to attend the wedding of his stepson John Park Custis to Benedict's daughter Eleanor.

The last of the Calverts to own Mount Airy were Dr. Cecilius Calvert and his sister, Eleanora Calvert. Both of them lived to an advanced age, and after their death the property, then composed of about six hundred and fifty acres, was sold. The house and grounds were acquired by Mrs. Matilda Roome Littell, who changed the name to Dower House. In 1908, she married Percival Duvall. She added the library and the music room to the north side of the house.

On February 1, 1931, a disastrous fire began in the domestic kitchen, gutting the old section and damaging the center hall and western wing. Mrs. Duvall moved to Washington and sold the house and eight hundred forty-four acres to Eleanor M. Patterson, a social leader and publisher of the Washington *Times-Herald*. She completely restored the mansion and was visited by many influential people, including President Franklin D. Roosevelt and General Douglas MacArthur.

Eleanor Patterson died in 1948, transferring the property to Anna Bowie Smith, a descendant of Eleanor Calvert Custis, and her husband Edward. They raised seven children and lived in the house until 1975, the last two years renting from the state of Maryland. In 1973, the estate of one thousand seventeen acres was purchased by the Department of Natural Resources and designated as Rosaryville State Park.

It was originally planned that Mount Airy would be the focal point of the park, and the Department did upgrade the interior. However, it was later decided to lease the mansion to a private firm for the purposes of development as a country inn.

The front door of the house gives on a hall running parallel with the front and rear porches. On the far side the stairway rises to the upper bedrooms. At the end is the door to the fine Colonial dining room from which a large kitchen opens. On the right, beyond a second staircase, is the old wing, now restored without changes to its original shape. A single great room takes up the center of the wing with a library on the right and a bedroom on the left. Small narrow dormer windows and inconsistently placed different colored bricks in the wall conjure up a perfect picture of the English countryside from which this type of small lodge would seem to have been transported bodily.

SNOW HILL

Route 197, Laurel

Set on a gradual slope not far from Laurel, about 400 yards from Montpelier, stands small, well-proportioned Snow Hill. It is one of the six Snowden Homes still standing. Others in that neighborhood included Birmingham Manor, Fairlands, Snowden's Hall, Montpelier and Oaklands. The last has a plan very similar to that of Snow Hill.

The original founder of this large and influential Colonial family was Richard Snowden of Birmingham, England, who first took up his residence in Maryland in 1658. His son, Captain Richard Snowden, owned "Robin Hood's Forest," which comprised some ten thousand acres of land, besides other great holdings. At one point, the total was 20,000 acres.

The Snowden grant was parcelled out in 500 acre lots as each descendant married and built their own home. Currently, Snow Hill stands on a 467 acre estate. The Snowdens were bankrupted by the Civil War, and now, of the entire 20,000 acre tract, no one in the family owns even one acre of the land.

Snow Hill, built about 1801, is the third house built on this site. It is a one and a half storey brick house with a gambrel roof and two chimneys. It is only thirty-five by fifty feet, not a large dwelling compared with Montpelier, but it seems surprisingly commodious. The front door, shaded by a small porch, opens into a rather narrow hall which runs through the house to the garden door.

The simple and modest stairway rises on the left of the hall. On the right, just inside the front door, is the entrance to the square parlor with its large fireplace flanked by cupboards. From this room a small, narrow stairway leads up to a second storey bedroom. The dining room, directly behind the parlor, is a little larger and has the same type of fireplace and cupboard arrangement. The left hand cupboard has been replaced by a door to the kitchen and pantry.

On the left of the hall there is a small bedroom which is gained by passing under the first landing of the stairs. Here the fireplace is in the corner. Behind the bedroom is the parlor, the largest room in the house, with a massive fireplace and a flanking rounded cupboard on the left.

As in many early homes, the original front is now the rear. In the golden days of river travel in the South, the main approach to a country house was from the water; and in this case the Patuxent River flows at the bottom of the hill not far away.

The present owner of Snow Hill is the widow of Dr. Bryan P. Warren, who purchased it in 1940 and fully restored it in the early 1950's. The Warrens have labored to preserve its ancient charms with loving hands and have complemented it with the finest of antique furnishings. Dr. Warren was the first doctor to treat Governor George Wallace when he was shot at Laurel Shopping Center in 1972.

There are many other well known houses in Prince George's County. Melwood Park, where George Washington often visited, is one of them, as is Harmony Hall, built about 1722, and named in 1793 by Mrs. Walter D. Addison, who was the daughter of Gustavus Hesselius, famous early Maryland portrait painter. Another dwelling older than the usual survivals of this pioneer era in Prince George's County is Mount Calvert Manor on the Upper Patuxent River. There is record that it was surveyed in 1653 for Robert Taylor, although the house probably was not built for some years afterward.

BRICE HOUSE

42 East Street, Annapolis

Brice House fronts on East Street, Annapolis, and is on the corner of Prince George Street, next to the Wm. Paca House. By reason of its great size and dignity and its immense chimneys which rise flush from the gable ends, the building stands out prominently. This great mansion was erected during the period of 1767 to 1773 by James Brice, who later was known as "the Colonel." John Brice, second, left his son, James Brice, lot number ninety-four in Annapolis and building materials "already worked up or to be worked up" to erect a dwelling house with outhouses.

James Brice's son, the Reverend Thomas Jennings Brice, inherited, willing the property at his death to his brother, Judge John Brice. The next owners were Nicholas Carroll Stephen and Charles W. Stephen. In 1873 Thomas E. Martin, Mayor of Annapolis, acquired the property. His descendents sold the property for the use of the Carvel Hall Hotel in 1911. In 1927 it was acquired by St. John's College.

Designated a National Historic Landmark in 1970, Brice House is a fine example of Georgian 5-part architecture. Laid in header bond, it measures 156 feet along a front terrace. The two and one-half storey central block, over an elevated basement, has chimneys towering 90 feet above the ground. The one and a half storey symmetrical wings and hyphens originally contained, in the east wing, the kitchen and children's schoolroom and the laundry and carriage house occupied the west wing.

The interior shows a sumptuous and exuberant display of superlative 18th century wood and plaster work. The entrance hall staircase is made of Santo Domingan mahogany, with plain balusters contrasted by an unusual molded handrail, columnar fluted newels, and elaborately carved rinceau brackets at each riser above a running fret. The dining room has a plaster cornice of full Corinthian entablature with a frieze of stylized honeysuckle vines, and a handsomely carved wood mantelpiece with elaborate side volutes. The ballroom features include magnificent cornice of full Corinthian entablature with richly carved modillions and rosettes and a swelled frieze of oak leaves and acorns, plaster panelled wall, chair rail with carved Greek key fret, and exceptionally finely-carved mantelpiece and overmantel. This elaborate work is repeated throughout the other rooms.

In 1953 Mr. & Mrs. Stanley Wohl acquired the Brice House and meticulously restored the exterior and preserved its elegant and distinguished interior plaster ornamentation and woodwork.

The building was acquired by Historic Annapolis, Inc. and a private group in 1983 for the purpose of assuring the protection of the fine interiors. The structure will be skillfully renovated as a small research and conference center for the International Masonry Institute. It will be opened to the public through Historic Annapolis, Inc.

CEDAR PARK

Cumberstone Road, Harwood

There are some sections of Maryland which suggest England more than others, and Cedar Park in Anne Arundel County lies in one of these. A rolling meadow dotted with huge old trees supplies a setting for one of the most remarkable homes of the state. This Queen Anne period house is situated on the West River and commands a fine view down the river to the Chesapeake Bay.

The original plan of the house is a thick-topped T, with a very steep pitched roof and narrow dormer windows. Enormous brick chimneys at either end emphasize the oddity of the gables. The brick work is a mixture of the all-header bond with English bond. In 1803, Governor John Mercer added an hexagonal drawing room or sitting room on the water side. Over this a large bedroom was added in 1820 so that there is a mixture of architectural styles which blend into a pleasing whole.

Great old trees and an English garden with high clumps of boxwood surround the house and provide a grateful shade on hot summer days. A large doorway on a long hall runs into the octagonal parlor. Doors to the right and left reveal narrow rooms with small fireplaces. The large dining room on the right and the master's bedroom on the left can be entered from the hall. In the master's bedroom is a small closet built into the wall, with iron bars across its tiny window, which might have been used for storing the family plate. The staircase rises on the left of the hall. A modern kitchen annex has been added on the right with a conforming roofline in keeping with the rest of the house.

As early as 1656, the estate was in the possession of Captain Richard Ewen, a Puritan Commissioner. A Patent for the property as Ewen upon Ewenton was granted in 1666. Richard Ewen's granddaughter Elizabeth Talbott married Benjamin Lawrence who acquired the Ewen Plantations in 1673. Upon his death in 1685, the land was held by English interests until Elizabeth, Benjamin Lawrence's widow, married Richard Galloway II, who purchased the property in 1697. Soon after this he built the present house according to his own design, enlarging and adding to it as his family grew.

Upon Richard Galloway's death in 1736, the property, then known as West River Farm, was inherited by his son Richard, Jr. When he died five years later the entire 2000 acre estate was left to his daughter Elizabeth, a Quakeress, who married Thomas Sprigg in 1746. They had but one child, Richard Sprigg. His daughter and heir, Sophia, married John Francis Mercer. The Mercers lived at Cedar Park until the property was deeded to their cousin, Fanny Cheston Murray, wife of Dr. James H. Murray, in 1869.

Ownership passed to his daughter Elizabeth, his grandson E. Churchill Murray and his great-granddaughter Marjorie who married Eveleth W. Bridgman, Jr., a cousin of Thomas Sprigg. The Bridgmans restored the house in 1961. After Marjorie died in 1975, Eveleth married Elaine Scott of Kent, England.

The present owners hope one of their children will mark the fourteenth generation of the same family to perpetuate the simple warmth, the timelessness and the proud remembrance of Cedar Park.

CHASE-LLOYD HOUSE

22 Maryland Avenue, Annapolis

Chase-Lloyd House in Annapolis, on the corner of King George Street and Maryland Avenue, bears the name of its two earliest owners, Samuel Chase and Edward Lloyd IV, both men of prominence in Maryland's history. This stately brick building is the only three storey house still standing in Annapolis which predates the Revolution. It is located across the street from the famous Hammond-Harwood House.

Though they each held ownership, Samuel Chase and Edward Lloyd IV were of vastly different backgrounds. Chase, the original owner, possessed ambition, competitive spirit, and political eagerness; he could boast of no immense family fortune unlike many of his comtemporaries. Chase became known for his legal skill and served many terms in the House of Delegates before President George Washington appointed him to the Supreme Court of the United States in 1796. By contrast, Edward Lloyd IV was a man of extreme wealth and social prominence. Lloyd was one of nine Marylanders who made up the "planter-lawyer aristocracy" which controlled Maryland's destinies during the Revolutionary period and after. Lloyd also owned the famous Wye House.

In 1769, Samuel Chase bought the land on Maryland Avenue from Denton Harwood. He had envisioned building a house "second only to that of Charles Carroll of Carrollton." Bound by financial restrictions, however, Samuel Chase was unable to complete his dream. In 1771, Edward Lloyd IV bought Chase's partially built mansion and exchanged additional property with Mathias Hammond to provide suitable grounds for the house.

Edward Lloyd, known as "Edward the Magnificent" because of his wealth and high standard of living, continued to build the dream Samuel Chase had conceived. The finished mansion was colossally opulent, a reflection of Lloyd's social position. Edward Lloyd IV went on to serve in the Continental Congress and was a member of the Convention of 1788 which ratified the Constitution. He entertained lavishly in his Annapolis home, one of his guests being Lafayette. Daughter Mary married Francis Scott Key, author of the national anthem, in 1802.

Lloyd IV died in 1796, at which time ownership of the house fell to his son, Colonel Lloyd. The house became the Governor's mansion in 1809 when Colonel Lloyd was elected to that office. In 1834, Governor Lloyd died. By that time, the family wealth had begun to diminish and family members had begun to scatter. Hester Ann Chase, second cousin of Samuel, bought the house in 1846, returning it to the original Chase family. Miss Chase lived there until her death in 1875. She willed the mansion to her three nieces, granddaughters of Samuel Chase. The last surviving niece, Hester Ann Chase Ridout, bequeathed the home to a Board of Trustees with the provision that the property be established as a home for aged and infirm women. In 1886, the Chase-Lloyd home became a home for elderly ladies, as it is to this day.

A flight of steps leads up the the white Palladian front door opening on a commodious columned hall. In the rear rises a beautiful staircase which divides into two flights halfway up. The dining room and parlor indicate the magnificent scale on which the Colonial gentry lived, for the locks and hinges are made of silver, the doors lined with mahogany, and the ceilings elaborately molded in stucco. Accordingly, the Lloyds displayed beautiful furniture and objects of art. Sculptured mantels of Italian marble grace many of the rooms, and the huge Palladian window at the landing of the stairs showed a fine disregard for the cost of glass. Even the inner sides of the interior wooden shutters are carved.

The walls of the house are eighteen inches thick and are composed of salmon colored brick laid in Flemish bond. The facade is unornamented, indicative of the spirit of its builder, while the luxurious interior reflects the taste of the second owner. To the right of the house is a small brick structure. It was the kitchen for the Chase-Lloyd House and is now a separate residence. In the rear and on each side of the palatial building is a large garden planted with exotic shrubs and flowers.

HAMMOND-HARWOOD HOUSE

19 Maryland Avenue, Annapolis

In Annapolis, on Maryland Avenue opposite the Chase House, is the Hammond-Harwood House, built between 1774 and 1776 for Mathias Hammond, attorney. The architect was William Buckland, designer of many other famous Annapolis and Maryland homes.

The brick dwelling is two storeys high with a central section and flanking wings, connected to the main building by one-storey "hyphens." The left wing contains the office; the right houses the kitchen and servants' quarters. The wings are semi-octagonal in shape. The front facade faces the street while the rear overlooks the remains of a once extensive garden.

According to tradition, Mathias Hammond started to build his home with the idea of marrying, and he determined to have the best house in Annapolis. However, stories relate that Mathias became so absorbed in the construction of the mansion that he neglected his fiancee, with the result she refused to marry him because she felt he cared more for it than he did for her. Mr. Hammond never married.

The Hammond-Harwood House has been for many years an inspiration to architects and historians studying the Colonial Georgian style. Its front doorway is undisputedly the finest Colonial entrance in America. The door is beneath a large rectangular window, above which is an aureole opening designed with the same fervor felt throughout the house.

The interior has rather small rooms which are exquisite in design and always symmetrical. The doors, window sills, mantels, wainscoting, panelling, and plasterwork are in perfect taste. The ballroom, nineteen by twenty-seven feet, on the second floor in the rear, is decorated with carvings. The rest of this floor is devoted to a game room and bedrooms.

When Mathias Hammond died in 1786, his nephew, John, inherited the property. Later John's brother, Philip, became the owner. Ninian Pinkney bought the house only to sell it a year later to Chief Justice Jeremiah Townley Chase, who gave it to his daughter Frances as a wedding gift when she married Richard Loockerman. Their eldest daughter wedded William Harwood, great-grandson of the architect, William Buckland. Of their four children, Hester Ann Harwood survived the others, but at her death in 1924 the treasures of the Hammond-Harwood House were dispersed at a dramatic auction sale. In 1926, St. John's College bought the house and planned to restore it as a museum of early Americana. When lack of funds prevented this, a group was formed called the Hammond-Harwood House Association, which has filled it with 18th century furnishings, including Peale portraits and Maryland furniture, and keeps it open to the public.

Mathias Hammond passed away almost two hundred years ago, but his dream, a perfect house, perpetuates his name.

OGLE HALL

247 King George Street, Annapolis

Ogle Hall was a residence of prominent political leaders of early Maryland, and has a long association with officers of the Navy. Now, fittingly, it is the home of the Naval Academy Alumni Association, and is also known as Alumni House.

Dr. William Stevenson died in 1739 just as he completed his plain but substantial two-story brick house. Soon afterwards the doctor's widow remarried, moved to the Eastern Shore, and offered her Annapolis house for rent. Samuel Ogle, Governor of Maryland, rented the house from 1747 until his death in 1752. His widow moved to the Ogle country estate of Bel Air and her brother purchased the Annapolis house for seventy tons of Baltimore pig iron. Mrs. Ogle subsequently acquired this city property and deeded it to her son Benjamin. While visiting Annapolis, George Washington entered in his diary on October 1, 1773 that he "dined with Mr. Ogle."

With the growing prosperity of Annapolis, a number of large Georgian mansions were built between the years 1765 and 1774. Accordingly, Benjamin Ogle undertook to embellish his home. His wife wrote her mother-in-law on February 5, 1776 "our House (is) in Confusion and Litter with Workmen and most of our furniture sent to Bel Air." It is likely that the extensive work done at this time included the addition of the ballroom wing, the cantilevered staircase, and possibly the three classical doorways including the jib-door. The balcony on the second floor is believed to be a much later addition. The existing "party wall" between the Chase-Lloyd House and Ogle Hall properties dates from 1774. According to tradition Lafayette visited Ogle Hall and planted a yew tree in the garden.

Benjamin Ogle served as Governor of Maryland from 1798 to 1801. James Steele purchased the house from the Ogle estate in 1815, his wife being related to the neighboring Lloyds. A son, Henry Maynadier Steele, married Maria Key, a daughter of Francis Scott Key. Henry and Maria's handsome Victorian house still stands at 248 King George Street.

Even before the founding of the Naval Academy, the Lloyd family had connections with the Naval service. Anne Catherine Lloyd had married Franklin Buchanan. When the Naval School (soon to be renamed the Naval Academy) was estalished in 1845, Commander Franklin Buchanan served as its first Superintendent. At this time his mother-in-law, Mrs. Edward Lloyd V, owned Ogle Hall.

Two years later the house was sold to retiring Maryland Governor Thomas Pratt. In 1868 he sold it to Judge and Mrs. John Thompson Mason, and again romance and marriage gave it added association with the Navy.

Following the Civil War, Vice Admiral David Dixon Porter became Superintendent of the Naval Academy and enrolled his son, Theodoric, as a midshipman. Admiral Porter made many important changes at the Academy including new buildings, new academic programs, more emphasis on athletics and social events, and the institution of the "June Week" tradition now known as "Commissioning Week." Midshipman Porter courted Bettie Mason of Ogle Hall. Three years after his graduation they were married. Theodoric Porter served forty three years in the Navy. During her husband's many years at sea, Bettie Mason Porter lived in Ogle Hall and raised a family. Commodore Theodoric Porter retired in 1908. In 1944 his daughter sold the house to the Naval Academy Alumni Association. The back porch shown in the etching has been removed by the Association, which does a marvelous job of preserving this historic structure.

PACA HOUSE AND GARDEN

186 Prince George Street, Annapolis

The Paca House and Garden first belonged to famous Maryland patriot William Paca. In keeping with other citizens of prominence during the eighteenth century, Paca chose Annapolis in which to build a house for himself and his bride, Mary Ann Chew. In addition to the well-appointed home, Paca also had a fine garden constructed for his wife, replete with rare flowers, an artificial brook, a bath house, and other unusual features. Today, the Paca House and Garden constitute one of Maryland's chief historic and architectural landmarks. The house stands on the same block with two other famous mansions of similar architecture: the Brice House and the Hammond-Harwood House.

William Paca chose the property at the time of his marriage in 1763. Paca lived there from 1765 when the mansion was completed until he sold it in 1780. During his years in Annapolis, Paca served on several councils, as a representative to the Continental Congress, and as a signer of the Declaration of Independence. He was also recognized for his distinguished service in the Revolutionary War. When the state government was inaugurated, Paca became a senator in the Maryland General Assembly. He later served three terms as Governor of Maryland, and was chosen a member of the Maryland convention which ratified the Constitution of the United States. Paca, a close friend of Annapolitan Samuel Chase, was also in contact with George Washington and other famous colonial citizens.

Thomas Jenings, a fellow attorney, bought the mansion from Paca in 1780. Following Jenings' death in 1796, his heirs rented the house to the Baron Henri de Stier. Throughout most of the nineteenth century, Paca House was used as a rental property. In 1907, a hotel building was attached to the north side of the house. The whole complex later became known as the Carvel Hall Hotel, so called because it was purportedly used as the setting for a popular romantic novel of that name written by American writer William Churchill. The hotel became widely known as a center of social activity among state legislators, Annapolis

visitors, and U.S. Naval Academy personnel. Though at one point Carvel Hall Hotel/Paca House was slated for demolition, it has been the focus of an extensive restoration process.

The large all-header brick Palladian-form mansion is located in the heart of the residential section of Annapolis. Set upon a five-foot brick terrace displaying an interesting variety of brick bonds, the Paca House is two-and-a-half storeys high, with large dormer windows and great chimneys flaring from either end. The house is covered by a steep gable roof, at the base of which is a simple box cornice. Two one-story wings are joined to the main portion of the building by passages. Each has had a complex architectural history; both wings have undergone extensive alterations during the mansion's two century existence.

The restored garden of the Paca House reflects the exquisite charm it held when William Paca had the area created for his wife. When Paca House became Carvel Hall, much of Paca's beautiful garden was destroyed. A Charles Wilson Peale portrait of William Paca reveals features of the garden in the background. Surrounded by a brick wall with ventilating slots, the garden contained an intricate irrigation system, a free-form sloped pond, and a spring house. The garden also held a Chinese Chippendale style bridge, an unusual two-story domed gazebo with urn shaped finials at each corner, and terraces with geometrically patterned borders. Today, the Paca Garden is destined to rank among the less than six eighteenth century gardens of the period in the country.

The interior of the Paca House retains much of its original woodwork. The famous drawing room, for example, contains a handsome chimney piece with a cornice shelf supported on a pulvinated frieze carved with oak leaves. Above the cornice shelf is a croisetted frame which has retained its original landscape painting. The cornice of the room is enriched with planter ornaments, and the window shutters are carved with octagonal motifs.

RIDOUT HOUSE

120 Duke of Gloucester Street, Annapolis

The Ridout House, one of the few Colonial dwellings in which the descendants of the original builder still live, faces east on Duke of Gloucester Street in Annapolis; its beautiful old garden even now is little curtailed by the growth of the city. John Ridout built the house in 1764 as a town residence and it was here, two years later, that he took his beautiful bride, Mary Ogle, daughter of Governor Samuel Ogle.

The building is not very large, being only two storeys high with small detached wings which give the impression of an enclosed court. Huge chimneys, almost as wide as the end of the building, rise well above the pitch of the roof while graceful trees shade the old salmon-colored bricks of the sidewalk. The gable roof is bare of dormer windows. A short flight of stairs, guarded by a wrought iron railing, installed in 1848, leads from the sidewalk to the pedimented Georgian doorway which opens directly on the hall. Off this hall are the doors leading to the dining room, the parlor, and in the rear, the study. In the parlor is one of the many treasures of the house, a harpischord given to Mary Ogle in 1764 by her cousin, Lady Essex. It is quite possible that Washington listened to the music made by the nimble fingers of the fair Mary as they lightly touched the keys. An unornamented stairway rises from the hall to the second floor. The entrance from the terraced garden, on the water side, is gained by a long flight of steps. The doorway is crowned by a great Palladian window, so large that it breaks the cornice of the house.

John Ridout was the friend and secretary of Governor Sharpe. He came to Maryland with the Governor in 1753 at the age of twenty-one, fresh from Oxford. Evidently he was a man of ability and greatly trusted by the Governor, for in 1757 he was given a mission to the Cherokee Indians which he successfully executed. His rise was rapid and three years later, mainly through Sharpe's influence, he became a member of the Governor's Council. Not only was he successful politically, but he also prospered financially until the Revolution.

Although a personal friend of Washington, John Ridout could not forget that he had been born an Englishman, and during the Revolution because of his Tory sentiments, was forced into seclusion at White Hall, his country home.

In 1797 John Ridout died, leaving three children, Samuel, Horatio, and Ann, the first of whom inherited the Ridout House. Samuel in 1790 had married Mary Grafton Addison, a relative of the famous English satirist. Since then the house has never been out of the Ridout family. Samuel's grandson, Dr. William Govane Ridout, died in 1914 leaving the property equally to Mrs. Charles Ligon, Mrs. C. Nelson Dugan, and the late Dr. John Ridout. The Ridout House is currently the home of Mr. & Mrs. Frederick G. Richards, Jr., the ninth generation of the Ridout family.

TULIP HILL

Route 468, Harwood

About one mile from Galesville, overlooking West River, stands Tulip Hill, the pride of Anne Arundel County. It was built by Samuel Galloway, who married Ann Chew in 1742 and built the house in 1756. According to an entry in the builder's account book all the bricks were made on the place.

The land originally was patented to Richard Talbot in 1659 as "Poplar Knowl." Washington "dined and supped" here twice in September, 1771. Samuel Galloway died in 1786, willing the house to his eldest son, John. At his death his only child, Mary Maxey, whose husband was Minister to Belgium, inherited. She left Tulip Hill to her daughter, Ann Sarah Hughes, who sold it to Henry M. Murray in 1886. His wife, Mary H. (Morris), was a descendant of the builder of the house. They lived there thirty years before selling to A. du Pont Parker, of Denver, Colorado. Tulip Hill then passed into the possession of Mr. and Mrs. Henry H. Flather, of Washington, D.C., who spent a great deal of time and patience in restoring the house and grounds to their Colonial magnificence.

The present owners, Mr. and Mrs. Lewis R. Andrews, bought Tulip Hill in 1948, and have lived there for the past thirty-five years, a longer period of time than any previous owner including the builder. Their avocation has been the restoration and preservation of this endearing pre-Revolutionary house, the gardens, and remarkable collection of ancient trees. Tulip Hill was designated a National Historic Landmark in 1970.

Tulip Hill stands on a ridge from which terraces paralleling the river lead down to the meadows. On these "falles" a beautiful garden was created in the last decade by the present owners. Two unusual brick chimneys, with multiple flues, project through either end of the central portion of the house and tower over the one storey wings.

The curious gambrel roof is set off by a pediment with its bull's-eye window. A well defined cornice and a small white pedimented porch with four columns shading the front door add dignity to the facade.

The spacious hall runs the depth of the house with a large double arch dividing it equally. The front half has a chair rail and a corner cupboard while the other half contains the staircase, up which one of the young Galloways is reputed to have ridden his horse. This portion of the hall has panelling to the ceiling and a three foot wainscoting up the stairs against the wall. The garden door has a famous hood which has been the inspiration of many architects. On the left of the hall are the doors to the parlor and the library, both large handsome rooms with beautiful mantels and panelling from floor to ceiling. These rooms rival the finest Colonial interiors in America. A door to the left leads to the last wing and a cozy sitting room with its separate fireplace.

On the right side of the hall is the door to the small estate office. The dining room may be entered from this room, or from the hall under the landing of the stairs. A door in the same relative position as in the west wing leads through the passageway to the kitchen. The present dining room was originally the housekeeper's room where supplies such as sugar, spices, and flour were measured out each day.

In the atmosphere of Tulip Hill people in modern dress are out of place. The story of a secret passage to the river does not seem incredible; even the skeleton who gallops about filling the night with unreasonably cheerful laughter does not seem an alien to Tulip Hill.

WHITEHALL

1915 Whitehall Road, Annapolis

Whitehall, seven miles southeast of Annapolis, is the first privately owned home in Maryland designated for the National Register. It is an outstanding example of a Georgian country house with the special distinction of being one of only two pre-Revolutionary houses in America to display a full temple portico. The salon of the main block along with the portico make Whitehall a unique example of Palladian architecture. Its grandeur and magnificence suggest a strong similarity to country dwellings of the English aristocracy. It provides an interesting illustration of the extension of this lifestyle into the Colonies by the royal governors.

Those who contributed to the building of Whitehall are among the most reknown of that period. It is likely that the famed William Buckland is responsible for the woodwork. John Rawlings mastered the plasterwork. Drawings of Whitehall are attributed to Joseph Horatio Anderson, one of the few professional architects of the Colonies.

The Whitehall mansion, consisting then of a central block, was built in 1764 for Governor Sharpe on a 1,000 acre estate overlooking the Severn River. At first, Sharpe used the central block as a retreat and for entertainment of guests coming down the river from Annapolis. Subsequently, Sharpe had the house enlarged, and it became his permanent residence when he retired in 1769. In 1773, Governor Sharpe went back to England and never returned. When he died in 1790 in London, Sharpe willed Whitehall to his one-time secretary and friend, John Ridout. The Ridouts added a second storey to the central block sometime around 1793. The family continued to own Whitehall until 1895, when Mrs. G.W. Story of Washington, D.C. acquired it. Today, Whitehall belongs to Mr. and Mrs. Charles Scarlett, Jr., who have painstakingly researched the history and architecture of the mansion to restore it to its 1769

appearance.

Whitehall is a five-part brick building of unusual length, about two hundred feet. The basement, exposed only on the north side, at one time held the Governor's office and dining room. On the main floor is a Great Hall, flanked by two rooms, and fronted by a portico of four great Corinthian columns. The north and south center doors each have semi-circular transoms topped by pediments.

The pedimented portico of the central block with its fluted columns is magnificent. The detailed, richly-carved exterior entablature suggests a Corinthian model shown in a famous English architecture text. The interiors of the main rooms contain elaborately carved woodwork, a trademark of William Buckland. Modillions, egg and dart ornament, and window casings with lateral consoles all bear a strong resemblance to similar details of Buckland's work in the Chase-Lloyd House and the Hammond-Harwood House in Annapolis. John Rawlings' elaborate plaster cornices are enriched with color and gilt.

By 1769, two brick wings were added to the central block with connecting one-storey arcaded passages. The current owners restored the mansion to this five-part form. The end wings each contain two bedrooms. Both are one storey high, though the wings seem like they are two storeys with their pyramidal roof and central chimneys.

Though John Ridout added a second storey to the house, the Scarletts removed it along with the 1793 gable roof and the added end pieces of the central block. The reconstruction involved rebuilding the gabled roof and balustrade to restore the central block to its former design.

The grounds have also been restored. Because Sharpe felt there was some danger of attack by Indians, he had constructed a sunken ditch, ramparts, and bastions on the land side.

CARROLLTON MANOR

Manor Woods Road, Frederick

Not far from the Darnell House and only a mile from Buckeystown is Carrollton Manor or Tuscarora, residence of Charles Carroll when he inspected his estates in the western part of Maryland. When the richest man in the colonies signed the Declaration of Independence in Philadelphia, he placed after his name "of Carrollton". It was from this Western Maryland property, an area reaching from the Potomac River and the Catoctin Mountains on the south and west to the foothills and Monocacy on the east, that he drew this title.

It is not known exactly when the house was built, but there is a record that Carroll was there in 1764, and has quarters for a retinue of slaves and stables for his horses.

Carrollton Manor is three storeys in height upon a high basement. It is constructed entirely of native limestone quarried on the property, except for the brick chimneys. Time has been so kind to the house, and the craftsmanship of its "mechanics" so thorough, it seems impossible that the building should date from the middle of the eighteenth century.

There are twenty-one rooms in Carrollton Manor, in addition to the divisions in the basement where a wine cellar and pantries for storing a plentiful supply of food and fuel were constructed. All the woodwork is of hardwood, carefully fitted and jointed.

The house is entered from a porch on the side and the front door opens on a reception hall. Opposite the foot of the stairs is the entrance to the large parlor with its huge folding doors which can be opened into the room behind to form a large ballroom. Both rooms are lighted by French windows which rise to the ceiling, with folding shutters in two sections. The fireplaces have flat oval columns supporting the mantels and, like all the woodwork, are severely plain. This absence of costly interior work suggests that Charles Carroll did not consider this home his permanent residence.

However, these details might have been improved by Robert Patterson, brother of the famous Betsy, who in 1820 married Mary Ann Caton, granddaughter of Charles Carroll, and moved to Carrollton Manor. As he hoped to make his home here he began extensive repairs and planned great porches around the whole building. Then cholera broke out in the countryside. The young bridegroom fled to Baltimore, but he was stricken and died a few days later. Mrs. Patterson took another husband, Richard Colley Wellesley, Marquis of Wellesley, Lord Lieutenant of Ireland, Governor General of India, and elder brother of Arthur, Duke of Wellington. It was turned over to tenants. The porches were allowed to fall into decay. None of the Carroll family ever lived there again.

When Charles Carroll died in 1832, his heirs were Mrs. Harper, the Marchioness of Wellesley, and members of the Lee, Jackson, and Tucker families. They owned Carrollton Manor until 1840, at which time some of the land was sold. In 1928 only twelve hundred acres remained in the possession of the Misses McTavish, direct descendants of the Carrolls. This property included the Manor Woods and the great old house, which then came into the hands of John and William Baker of Buckeystown. Carrollton Manor is now owned by the Eastalco Aluminum Company. It has been restored to good condition and is maintained that way by the company. It has been occupied by Eastalco managerial employees since its purchase in 1968.

FAT OXEN

Route 355, Urbana

A third of a mile from Urbana, just off Maryland Route 355, stands Fat Oxen, one of the oldest homes in Frederick County. Fat Oxen has served as the home of many influential citizens of the county. It is a good example of a mid-18th century English farmhouse built in an area largely settled by Germans and where most of the surviving structures are of German character.

The first English settlers located in the Urbana area sometime around 1740. William Beall, Sr. acquired a 1,000 acre tract of land called Fat Oxen at some point before 1754. Though it had been divided into many parts, the property stayed in the Beall family until 1800. When Joseph Beall sold 285 acres of the tract to Charles Beall in 1779, the deed indicates that the land included "a dwelling plantation."

In 1800, a group of Beall heirs sold Fat Oxen to Thomas Sprigg, a member of the illustrious Sprigg family of Prince George's County. After Sprigg died in 1926, John McPherson, Sr. bought the estate at public auction. Ownership then fell to John McPherson, Jr. when his father died. For the next 100 years, Fat Oxen belonged to the McPherson, Dennis, and Ross families, all related. These families made overwhelming contributions to Frederick County and Maryland history. They were responsible for directing plans for the National Pike, and family members held numerous state and government positions.

Today, Fat Oxen is occupied by farm tenants.

Fat Oxen is an unpretentious brick house, laid in Flemish bond. The house rises from a knoll one-and-one-half storeys over a high stone foundation. The kitchen wing is attached to the southeast elevation and is also one-and-a-half storeys. Both the main block and the wing are unusually deep for a house of this scale. Fat Oxen is basically Georgian vernacular in style.

The five bays wide house has two double parlors with a partially open center hall. The wing is two bays wide. A high wooden mid-19th century porch shaded the two doors until it was removed in 1976. The doorway in the third bay is original. Two period dormers sit on the gradually-pitched roof. Central enclosed chimneys stand at each end of the house.

The interior of Fat Oxen has been altered many times during the last two centuries. Woodwork from every period can be found inside. Much of the woodwork is notable, including beaded chair rails, baseboards, and flat panelled shutters in the window reveals and interior doors. Each of the four main rooms in the central block have back to back corner fireplaces. The mantels are rare, as the raised panelling over face design continues down only one side of the fireplace opening. The chimneys are rare, as well, as they are asymmetrically placed along the roof ridge line. The staircase, which rises on the left, has heavy molded handrails and simple rectangular balusters. A heavy chair rail runs across the stair landing and continues to the second floor level.

On the second floor are four very simple rooms of windows in the gable ends. Random width pine boards cover the floor.

The basement area remains intact as an original cellar of the period. A wooden stairway descends to the dirt floor. Original plank cellar partitions and sorting bins stand in the southeast half of the basement, making it an interesting study for architectural historians and archaeologists, alike.

ROSE HILL MANOR

1611 North Market Street, Frederick

A mile north of Frederick, close to the main road to Gettysburg, is the large white Georgian home known as Rose Hill. Thomas Johnson, a close political associate as well as personal friend of George Washington, and the first elected Governor of Maryland, purchased 225 acres of the 7000-acre Tasker's Chance tract in 1778. In 1788, he gave the land to his daughter, Ann Jennings Johnson, while he continued to reside on his estate known as Richfields.

In 1793, Miss Johnson and her husband, Major John Grahame, started building Rose Hill, and it was completed in 1798. After the death of his wife, Governor Johnson left Richfields and joined the Grahame household. Governor Johnson lived at Rose Hill until his death in 1819. The Grahames occupied Rose Hill until the Major's death in 1833.

During the nineteenth century, the house had several owners, including John McPherson, who operated the Catoctin Iron Works. In 1906, title passed to Noah E. Cramer, a successful businessman who modernized the house.

The white painted brick mansion is approached by a driveway which divides as it passes through the entrance gates and curves in a circle to the front steps. The large two storey porch supports a graceful pediment with a half-moon in its tympanum. Two dormer windows project from the roof of the main building, but there is none on the small two storey left wing.

The large front door opens into a spacious hall dividing the main wing into two equal parts. On the right is the state ball room with an impressive plaster moulding. This room is twenty-two by twenty-seven feet, with a rather small projecting fireplace and mantel, and six large windows. In recent years two ornamental columns have been added to the entrance and the door has been removed.

Opposite the doorway to the ball room is the entrance to the great dining hall, where the dimensions are the same as the ball room. There is also a projecting fireplace. In the right hand corner beside the mantel is the door to the kitchen and the servants' wing. This is composed of two rooms and has its own staircase.

The main stairway rises half way down the hall on the left. Under the first landing is the door to the small garden porch, which is pedimented.

Rose Hill is a fine example of Georgian symmetry and simplicity. The main section is an almost exactly balanced whole, as is the servants' wing.

The grounds surrounding the mansion are beautifully kept, and here a very old cherry tree still bears fruit. On the left of the house is a curious building with a sunken basin which is five feet deep, four feet wide and seven feet long. This is reputed to have been the bath tub of Governor Thomas Johnson.

Rose Hill is now a public museum. It is open 7 days a week (10 a.m. to 4 p.m. Monday through Saturday and 1 p.m. to 4 p.m. on Sundays) from April through October. Rose Hill is open on weekends only in March, November and December, and closed in January and February.

HAGER'S CHOICE

19 Key Street, Hagerstown

In Hagerstown, a short distance from the Washington County Museum, across the railroad tracks, stands the reputed home of Jonathan Hager, founder of Hagerstown. The original grant was made in 1739, and the house looks as if it were erected soon after this time. In those days the Indians were a real danger and every dwelling had to be planned with the idea of defense in mind. To insure the water supply in case of siege, Hager's Choice was built over two springs, one feeding the other.

Situated in a little dell between hills, the house is constructed of uncut stone carefully fitted. Hand hewn beams span the basement where an enormous fireplace is ready to take the chill from the damp air with a cheery blaze. The floors and window sills are of walnut. A forerunner of modern insulation of walls and floors was practiced in this house where a composition of rye straw and mud fills the space between the beams, making the house cool in summer and warm in winter.

Hager's Choice is two-and-a-half storeys high with a large basement and an attic. As in most of the early settlers' homes in Western Maryland, there are no dormer windows and only one chimney. Here the chimney rises through the middle of the dwelling and is topped with brick. When the house was first erected it was only one-and-a-half storeys, but since then the roof has been raised and more rooms added. However, this must have been in the middle of the eighteenth century, for the construction is much the same as in the original building.

The house is entered from the porch, reached either from the side of the hill or by a flight of steps on a lower level. A deeply recessed door shows the thickness of the stone walls, and gives on an entrance hall partitioned off since the original plan was laid out. On the left a small corner staircase winds up to the second floor, while a door to the front room opens on the right. When one goes through the temporary partition to the room in the rear, one finds a peculiar small cupboard set in the back of the chimney. This is said to have been used to store wood for fuel. Opening on the right wall, is a door to the third room on the first floor. All these rooms have a small chair rail and rough plaster laid on the stone itself. On the second floor is a heavy built-in cupboard with a rat-tail hinge. Strap and HL hinges are found throughout the house.

The atmosphere of Hager's Choice is entirely different from that found in the Eastern Shore and Southern Maryland homes. The house is more a fort and less a dwelling. The pioneers who lived in Western Maryland knew that they carried their lives in their hands, and built accordingly. Naturally the mountainous terrain and the building material available exerted some influence. Where a place of refuge had to be constructed without a delay of months, it took too long to make bricks, so that the very early houses were either of logs or of rough stones.

The house, now owned by the City of Hagerstown, has been furnished in a manner appropriate to the times. It is open to the public from 10-5 p.m. except Monday from May 1 through September. Sunday, the hours are 2-5 p.m. On the grounds, there is also a museum with items dealing with the Hager family and the early history of Hagerstown.

LANCELOT JACQUES HOUSE

Route 56, Big Spring

Three miles south of Clear Spring, at Green Spring Furnace, is located a log and clapboard house built before 1750 by Lancelot Jacques, a French Huguenot refugee, who came to America and became a great friend of Thomas Johnson, later Governor of Maryland. Together they operated Catoctin Furnace and were partners in many business ventures, not dissolving partnership until 1776. Lancelot Jacques kept the Green Spring property and his nephew, Denton, lived there after him.

The house was admirably situated for defence against the Indians, as it was on a hill close to a fine spring. Three miles southwest was Fort Frederick, offering refuge if the attack on the dwelling proved too much for the small group of pioneers to cope with. When Braddock marched to his death he passed near here, camping under Fairview Mountain.

Lancelot Jacques House is made up of three sections. One is a one-and-a-half storey hipped roof wing with dormer windows and an enormous chimney of dressed stone. This is laid up in regular courses which are divided into three equal parts by two set-backs in somewhat the same manner as the modern skyscraper. This part of the house has a stone foundation, with thick walls of logs covered by clapboard and is joined at right angles to the main building, two storeys high and clapboarded. A hall runs through the house and the stairs are on the right beyond the door to the parlor. This room is almost square and has a chair rail about it; there is also one in the hall. The sitting room is located across from the parlor.

Separated from the main building and on a lower level is a log cabin. This is one of the few buildings still standing which follow the construction principles of pioneer dwellings as described by contemporary writers. The logs are dovetailed together with no nails or pegs to hold them in place. The cabin has a basement entered by a double door so sturdy that it might have come from a medieval castle. A huge fireplace of stone provided heat and firelight. The windows are very small. Upstairs the arrangement is simple. There is a partition dividing the house into two rooms, each one with an outside door. The steps to the low pitched attic are unassuming. There are no signs of panelling or plaster as this was a true pioneer cabin.

The main building is more pretentious, and it is possible that the cabin was used only as a trading store and fort. At the time Lancelot Jacques settled at Green Spring Furnace he owned fifteen thousand acres in the neighborhood. Today there are only one hundred and thirty acres in the property, as Interstate 70 has taken land away. Much of the acreage is now used as pasture. The present owner is Andrew J. Michael, who purchased the property in 1959.

LONG MEADOWS

Marsh Pike, Hagerstown

Long Meadows, the residence of Judge and Mrs. Daniel W. Moylan, is a significant name in the history of Washington County. It is about four miles north of the city of Hagerstown, but within its postal area. The 30-room yellow brick and stone house is an architectural complex that evolved from a one-room stone cottage built in the early eighteenth century by an unknown settler.

Long Meadows is closely connected with the Cresap family. After Colonel Thomas Cresap moved from the neighborhood of Havre de Grace, he settled in 1739 at Long Meadows Farm on 500 acres of land and built a fort of stone and log to protect one of the earliest settlements in the county. He borrowed 500 pounds from Daniel Dulaney, first Attorney General of Maryland, and started in business, but failed when a shipload of furs which he was sending to England was captured by the French. To liquidate his debt to Dulaney, Cresap turned over his Long Meadows property and in 1746, moved further west to Oldtown.

Dulaney added a land grant of his own, increasing the tract to 2,131 acres. Colonel Henry Bouquet, a British army officer in the French and Indian War, purchased it in 1763, and increased the tract to over 4,000 acres. Col. Bouquet is known for defeating the Indian chief Pontiac in the Battle of Bushey Run, and for establishing a major east-west road through western Pennsylvania.

In the course of time, the acreage decreased in transactions with succeeding owners. In 1773, the tract was purchased by General Joseph Sprigg, who fought in the Revolutionary War. He was followed by Samuel Hughs, owner of the Mount Aetna Furnace and a member of the Maryland Legislature, in 1779. It was Hughs who was instrumental in having the county named for George Washington.

In 1789, it became the property of Colonel Thomas Hart, a wealthy merchant who was a business partner of Nathaniel Rochester of Hagerstown. Rochester was the founder of the city of Rochester in upstate New York. Col. Hart's daugher, Lucretia, became the wife of statesman Henry Clay.

Thomas Hall, a government tax collector, purchased the property in 1794. He later absconded with public funds, and Long Meadows was taken over by the Federal Government. In 1831, it was sold at public auction to Dr. Richard Regan. In 1887, it was sold to William Young of Baltimore, and Long Meadows remained in the Young family until 1974, the year before Moylans acquired it in 1975. At that time, it was listed as a 210-acre farm, but the Moylans purchased only the house and four acres, while the developer who acquired it from the Young family is farming the remaining acreage.

The first addition to the stone cottage was a two-story frame section, that was later torn down in 1908. About 1840, a spacious brick section, with a broad central hall, was joined. This was completed during the Regan ownership.

It was the Young family who tore down the early frame addition and rebuilt it in brick to match the 1840 section in 1908. The architect involved was H.E. Yessler of York, Pennsylvania, who had designed several important houses in Hagerstown. Interior alterations to the stone cottage and the extension of four rooms on the north side were completed in 1936.

The Moylans have also accomplished a lot in the restoration process, rewiring, plumbing, plastering and painting, as well as tastefully furnishing the house in period pieces and accessories. Judge Moylan's father, the late Judge Charles Moylan of the Baltimore Supreme Bench, was a collecter of antique furniture.

The main entrance opens to the 1840 section, embracing the library, music room and stair hall, which separates equally spacious drawing and dining rooms in the remodeled 1908 section. A butler's pantry is transitional to the stone wing containing a large country kitchen and an adjoining den with a beautiful fireplace wall of panelled walnut. The second floor consists of the master bedroom and sitting room, four children's rooms and several guest rooms.

MICHAEL CRESAP HOUSE

Main Street, Oldtown

In 1709, at the age of fifteen, there came to Maryland from Skipton-in-Craven, England, one Thomas Cresap, who later achieved the title of Colonel. He married Miss Hannah Johnson, April 30, 1727. This union resulted in three sons, Daniel, Thomas, and Michael. Daniel was a steady, hard working farmer who became well known in Allegany County. He built a stone house at Rawlings, in which Governor Lloyd Lowndes afterward lived. Thomas was killed in an Indian fight.

However, it is with Michael Cresap that this account is principally concerned. He was a high spirited young man who grew up in the atmosphere of his father's fort, which stood on a rise of ground only a short distance from Oldtown, originally an Indian village, on the banks of the Potomac. Michael was born June 29, 1742, and survived the Indian raids which threw Annapolis into panic. He must have met Washington, as the General stayed at Colonel Cresap's fort on several occasions.

Michael Cresap was the first Captain commissioned in the Revolutionary War by the State of Maryland. In June, 1775, he left Allegany County with his men and marched north to join Washington's army there. He had been ill before he left on the journey. After his arrival in Massachusetts, he grew worse and was removed to New York City, where he died October 18, 1775, at the age of thirty-three. His body lies in Trinity Churchyard.

It is peculiar that a man should be remembered for the things he did not do, but in Captain Cresap's case this is true. He was blamed by Jefferson as being the instigator of Dunmore's War with the Indians, on the charge of having murdered the family of Logan, a prominent Indian chief. However, the consensus is that Captain Cresap was wrongly accused. Even in his day this must have been realized, as he was commissioned a Captain in the Revolutionary Army after the alleged murders.

Captain Cresap was married August 4, 1764; and his home was probably built soon after this. At any rate it was standing in the summer of 1774, as Lord Dunmore visited him then and spent several days. It is the oldest structure in Oldtown and was once used for the town jail, as the cell in the basement testifies.

The house is of rough stone and is taller than its two storeys would indicate, due to the high basement. The panelled front door, with a porch before it, is reached by a flight of steps along the house wall. Opening directly into the parlor, the front door, which is hung on massive hand-wrought hinges, seems to have been constructed to withstand not only the assaults of human enemies, but of time as well.

In line with the front door is the opening to the back room, from which the enclosed stairs rise on the right to the upper storey. In both the parlor and the back room there is a chair rail and a fireplace, flanked by large double cupboards. On the ceiling of the second storey there used to be a frescoe of dogs, deer, and guns, but this work of art was covered over by later owners until the outlines of it are barely discernible.

The Cresap name is one of the most noted in Maryland history, and the family, still prominent in America, has insured its solidarity by the formation of the Cresap Society. The members of this organization have erected a monument to Colonel Thomas Cresap in the Oldtown Community Park. The Michael Cresap House is now a public museum owned by the Allen Family Corporation.

OLD KING FARM

Kings Road, Ellerslie

Just outside the town of Ellerslie, close to the Pennsylvania boundary line, is Old King Farm, originally called "Rural Felicity", reputed to have been erected in 1793 by Benjamin Tomlinson. A more beautiful site could not have been chosen for the first brick dwelling in Allegany County. Green clad mountains rise on both sides of the valley giving evidence of God's creative hand; a branch of Wills Creek flows nearby.

There is no doubt that the bricks of this house were made on the farm and that the stones for the foundation cellar running under the whole structure were gathered from the surrounding fields. The original house contained only three rooms, but later a hall and other rooms were added using the same type of brick, so that the two-and-a-half storey building with its three large brick chimneys jutting from the roof remains a harmonious whole.

There are two back doors, one opens directly into a large dining room with a fireplace on the left, and cabinethead archway leading into a large living room with double fireplaces on the right. These rooms have ceilings and moulding of hand-planed wood. A front door opens onto a two storey porch, with four square columns rising to a gable roof. The second back door opens into the hall from which rise the stairs to the upper floors. The stairway has none of the flourishes often found in southern manor houses. On the left of the hall is the kitchen and entry way to the basement. The fireplace is against the left wall but it has been closed up. In this room as well as in all the others on the first floor, the only adornment is a chair rail, and the smallness of the twelve-paned windows bear witness to the high cost of glass in those days.

The exterior of the house has a wide wooden cornice under the eaves. There has been no effort to plant a formal garden, but the beauty of the surroundings is such that any attempt to improve on nature would impair the repose and simplicity of the homestead.

There are two family cemeteries on the farm. Reading the epitaphs one realizes their belief in God is evident, by the testimony they left behind. America's Godly heritage is reflected by such people as these.

From the Tomlinson family the farm passed through marriage to the possession of Alexander King. Several generations of the Kings owned the farm until the early 1920's. The farm was purchased in 1959 by R. Joseph and Janet Lybarger and has been restored to a working farm, which Joe operates along with his son J. Andrew Lybarger, his wife and children.

The Lybarger family seeks to carry on the tradition of such God-fearing families that are the spiritual fiber that has always undergridded our republic. America was founded upon a firm belief in God and built upon that truth.

VALE SUMMIT

Frostburg

In the coal mining region outside of Frostburg lies the property known as Vale Summit, also called Pompey Smash. Most of the early homes in this region were constructed of stone and were rather crude, but upon Vale Summit once stood a large two-storey mansion with a smaller two-storey wing. Obviously, this had been the residence of a man of means and taste.

It is related that Captain William Lamar, born in Frederick County in 1755, and having served with the Continental Army, erected the mansion immediately following the Revolutionary War. Captain Lamar resided at Vale Summit until his death in 1838. His grave remains under a large tree near the house, but his tombstone has been relocated to Rose Hill Cemetery.

Following Lamar's death, a Mr. Kirby took over the farm's operation until after the Civil War. Mr. Kirby completed the mansion by erecting the smaller two-storey addition that was used as servants' quarters.

A low narrow chimney rose from the main section while a smaller one indicated a fireplace in the kitchen. A wooden porch crossed the front of the house with a pedimented break over the door. A small porch covered the entrance to the servants' quarters.

The front door was panelled about the casing and continued into a semi-circle hooding the glass fanlight. The hall, lined with a chair rail, ran the depth of the house to the rear door opening onto a large back porch. Halfway down the hall an arch interrupted; a stairway lay beyond. The stairway, with a walnut hand rail, rose to the upper story and attic. The first door on the right of the hall opened to a spacious living room. Over this door was a carving attributed to Hessian soldiers. A large fireplace with a built-in cupboard on the left dominated the room. Behind it was a slightly smaller chamber, also with a fireplace. Upstairs, the mantels were almost identical to those on the lower floor. The wing contained a small dining room and kitchen. The fireplace in the wing also had a built-in cupboard to its left.

The house derives its primary name from the land's highest point, Vale Summit. Its nickname has a peculiar origin. Pompey Smash is so called in honor of Pompey (one of Kirby's slaves) who, on an errand for his master, overturned in the mule-drawn wagon. The men of the village later gathered in the tavern and, laughing over Pompey's distress over his fear of punishment from his master, nicknamed the land Pompey Smash.

Since the days of Pompey, a coal mining company has bought and utilized Vale Summit for strip mining. All that remain are the foundation walls and the kilns in which the building's bricks were fired.

THE DRANE HOUSE

Accident-Bittinger Road, Accident

At Accident, in a plateau valley, is a frontier home containing six rooms (three on the first floor, three on the second floor), a log-frame combination covered with clapboard, now the property of Clark and Marvin Kolb. This quaint reminder of pioneer days was built when the original member of the Drane family came to Garrett County, at that time a haunt for Indians and considered unsafe for settlers. It is the oldest standing log-frame combination home in Garrett County.

James Drane, Jr. was born in 1755 in Prince George's County, and in 1779 was commissioned Second Lieutenant in the Middle Battalion of his county. He married Priscilla Lamar of French Huguenot descent, and lived in Prince George's County before moving to Accident. It would appear that James Drane never held the title to the property, as it belonged equally to his wife and her brother, William Lamar, who also owned Vale Farm near Frostburg.

When the Drane family moved there, it was a heavily wooded area near some bear dens. These animals were sometimes a menace, though according to records, only once did a bear actually come to the Drane house. They were little black bears, hardly as dangerous as portrayed. Members of the Society of Friends who settled nearby, claimed to have killed over seventeen, however, during their first year of residence. Meschach Browning, whose autobiography is one of the famous documents of that period, gives much space to the stories of these beasts. However, James Drane was not daunted, and he lived and prospered there until his death in 1828, survived by his wife and eight children.

When James Drane moved to Western Maryland from Prince George's County, he continued planting tobacco with slave labor, but the venture was not highly successful as the market was too far away and the soil became exhausted too quickly. The short growing season also contributed to the failure. (Though it had been one of the principal crops of this section, very little tobacco was being raised by the time the Germans began arriving in 1842). At his death, Drane left six slaves, valued at $1,450.00 and $191.78 in other effects. The inventory was signed by John McHenry and Meschach Browning.

The house is located east of Accident, one-fourth mile off Route 219. By turning onto the Accident-Bittinger Road you can travel eastward, and watching closely near the large farm barn, the house can be located among the maple trees. The Drane home reflects the contrasting conditions faced by the men who opened up the West and those who came from England to take up great estates along the Chesapeake.

The original one-and-a-half storey two-room dwelling, to which has been made a three-room addition, was probably built about 1800. Today it rests on stones on the ground (there is no cellar) and the outside walls are shedding the insul covering, exposing the wide boards which covered the logs from the time it was made ready for the Drane family. The chimney, made of field stone, toppled in 1970. The low porch deteriorated under heavy snows of 1983.

The rooms are small but surprisingly well-lighted. No panelling, chair rails, or plaster moulding can be found inside. Originally, the walls were chinked with mud. Later, boards of varying widths were nailed over the logs, and still later, wallpaper was placed over the boards. Wide steps lead to the second floor, where the rooms are as large as those below them, though they are very poorly lighted. Beside the large room there is a kitchen where a cook stove was used by later residents. It is believed that the big room served as dining room, living room, and kitchen for the Dranes. The old fireplace has been boarded up. Thick walls make the house cool in summer, and in winter shut out the chill blasts sweeping across the Allegheny Mountains.

The Drane House is in need of some restoration. Yet descendents still return to see their ancestral homestead.

CHERRY GROVE

17530 New Hampshire Avenue, Ashton

Years ago, a community known as Sandy Spring existed as a self-sufficient group of the Society of Friends in Montgomery County. For a time, an elected historian kept detailed records of community activities. "The Annals of Sandy Spring" is a twenty-year diary of this neighborhood, describing the triumphs and struggles of its residents. Cherry Grove is one of the interesting homes whose early inhabitants were once a part of this close-knit group.

The original building was erected in 1728. Destroyed by fire in 1773, Cherry Grove was reconstructed immediately by owner Richard Thomas. It was at this time that the place was named Cherry Grove after the cherry orchard which Mr. Thomas planted on the property.

The Thomas family owned Cherry Grove for many generations. It was in 1925 when Samuel Thomas lost the mortgage to the house that ownership of the property fell to a Washington-based real estate company. Roger Brooke Farquhar and his wife, Jean, bought Cherry Grove in 1928 from Hewitt Real Estate. The couple ran what might have been called a "country restaurant" until Prohibition ended. The Farquhars also changed the name to Brooke Manor Inn during their ownership. In 1945, Mr. and Mrs. George H. Riggs bought Brooke Manor and renamed it Cherry Grove. They remain owners of the house.

Cherry Grove is a fine example of Colonial architecture, though it has been renovated many times in the interest of convenience. The basic lines of the house remain unchanged, however.

Originally, the kitchen wing was more of a dependency. There was a breezeway between it and the main house. Until close to 1860, the kitchen was a one-storey wing, but the Thomases added another level to accommodate their family. They also eliminated the breezeway to attach the wing directly to the main house. The wing had a flat tin roof until the Farquhars had a ridge roof built during their ownership. Beneath the hardwood kitchen floor, a well once existed.

The front door opens onto a commodious hall with stairs on the right. At the back of the hall is the entrance to a sitting room with a panelled fireplace and two panelled-door cupboards on the left. Interestingly, this room originally held a large closet with shelves to the left of the fireplace, an unusual feature for a house of the period. Later, when the owners rented out part of Cherry Grove, they enlarged the closet area and added a window to convert it to a bathroom. Notable, too, is the asymmetrical panelling around the room. In the eighteenth and nineteenth centuries, panelling was erected simply to fit the necessary spaces, usually without regard to evenness and symmetry. Other renovations to the room included the addition of an elaborate Adams style fireplace with a mantel shelf. Initially, the fireplaces throughout Cherry Grove were generally built to one side, near the inner wall, and none had a mantel shelf.

The first door on the left leads to the living room, with a fireplace facing the door. There are cupboards on either side. Walls are panelled, floor to ceiling. In order to get to the room once used as a dining room, the Thomases had one of the living room cupboard spaces converted into a doorway so that their boarders would have access to it. This room has a smaller, arched fireplace.

CLIFTON

17107 New Hampshire Avenue, Ashton

Somnolently resting beneath the shade of a grove of trees is Clifton, c. 1740, one of the oldest documented houses in Sandy Spring, Md., a community settled by Quakers in 1728. The Thomas family built the house and lived in it for over 200 years. They still have the original deed to the property in their possession. They were members of the Sandy Spring Friends Meeting and were generous contributors to the construction of the present Meetinghouse, built in 1817.

Clifton is constructed of brick laid in the flemish bond pattern with a thick soapstone foundation. The main part is two storeys high with an attic, gambrel roof, and three dormer windows. A small one and a half story wing, added in 1846, is on the left. The home is a short distance from Cherry Grove, another Thomas house.

There is a friendly atmosphere about this old home which holds forth an invitation to the traveller. The front door opens on a rectangular entrance hall. A wide low door under the landing of its generous and beautiful original stairs leads to the basement. On the right of the hall is a door to the lovely old-fashioned garden. On the left is the entrance to the parlor in which there is an original built-in corner cupboard. Across another corner is the fireplace, panelled to the ceiling. Directly behind the parlor is the sitting room where the corner fireplace connects with the same flue as the one in the parlor.

In the wing is the dining room and kitchen. In the far corner of the dining room is a narrow flight of winding stairs leading to the attic-like rooms over this part of the house. The kitchen, modernized by the present owners, incorporates the old summer kitchen fireplace, formerly in an adjacent shed.

The present owners, James and Elizabeth Bullard, also members of Sandy Spring Friends Meeting, have lived in the house for 17 years and are slowly restoring it. The house was documented by the Historic American Buildings Survey in 1936 and is on the National Register of Historic Buildings.

This section of Montgomery County is the one in which the famous Sandy Spring settlement of Friends was situated. It has been said that the farmers were so thrifty here that there was only one pair of boots in the neighborhood, which was loaned whenever a member of the community wished to go to town.

Near Clifton is Falling Green, where Miss Mary Brook and Mrs. W.F. Green, her sister, live. They are the seventh generation and direct descendants of Basil Brook, who built the original house in 1762. This dwelling has high fireplaces with narrow wooden mantels. The hall is in the centre of the structure and the large parlor, where there is wainscoting to three feet, has been partitioned. In the dining room is a ceiling-high built-in cupboard flanking the fireplace.

There are so many of the old Thomas homes in and around Sandy Spring that one historian was moved to remark, "The Thomases were builders and most of the brick buildings in the locality are monuments to them."

NORWOOD

Norwood and Dr. Bird Roads, Sandy Spring

Not far from Sandy Spring at a very sharp turn to the right in the main road is the entrance to Norwood, another Thomas homestead. Built in 1741 by Samuel Thomas, for many years this charming dwelling remained in the family, finally passing into the possession of the Scotts.

Norwood stands in its own grounds with fine lawns surrounding it on three sides and on the other, what the elements and time have left of a great boxwood maze. When an enormous weeping willow tree fell some years ago, it crushed more of the boxwood. Wood carvers immediately rushed from Washington and Baltimore to buy the scarce willow wood, as that is the best material out of which to make artificial legs.

The building is of brick with a stone foundation. A large cellar runs under the main structure. The kitchen, in what was once a one-and-a-half storey wing, is very much like Clifton, except that the roof has been raised until now the line is level with the main section of the house. When the dwelling was remodelled in 1867, the windows were enlarged a foot, as the uncentered old arch above them testifies.

The front door opens under this stairway and leads into a hall which bisects the main building. This contained the living quarters of the Thomas family. At the foot of the stairs is the door to the living room where two fireplaces reveal that a partition has been removed. Opposite the parlor door is the entrance to the dining room, repanelled in 1922 after the old pattern, which had been removed by former tenants of the house. Large double doors open into the library which also can be entered from the hall. The panelling here was replaced at the same time as that in the dining room. The rooms on the second floor are very cozy and there are fireplaces in each of them. An old iron fireback in one bedroom bears the date 1751 under entwined hearts.

For several years Philip E. Thomas, son of Evan Thomas of Mt. Radnor, lived at Norwood. He was the first president and guiding force of the Baltimore and Ohio Railroad. However, in spite of being able at one time to advance money to help in building the Washington Monument, he later lost most of his wealth, and had to retire to the country.

In 1867 Joseph T. Moore bought Norwood from Samuel Weller. His daughter, Margaret C. Moore, married Milton H. Bancroft in 1893. Mr. Bancroft and his son, both well known artists, lived at Norwood.

It remained in the Bancroft family until 1979, after the 1978 death of John T. Bancroft. The property was divided and the house with 11 acres was purchased by Mr. and Mrs. Christian Domergue, the present owners.

Legend has it that two ghosts inhabit Norwood. One is said to be that of a black woman who had lived there thirty-five years and refused to leave after she died. The second legendary spirit has not been identified, but whenever Mrs. Joseph T. Moore, who suffered from insomnia, walked up and down the halls late at night, the rustling of a ghostly silk dress accompanied her steps.

CLYNMALIRA MANOR

Carroll Road, Monkton

Not far from Monkton in Baltimore County stands Clynmalira, a large mansion, the original dimensions of which are considerably increased by modern porches on two sides. In 1707, when Charles Carroll was granted the five thousand acres which made up the original tract, it was all wilderness. This land descended to Daniel Carroll of Duddington on the death of the first owner. When Daniel Carroll passed away, the heir was Charles Carroll, Jr., who in turn left Clynmalira to Henry King Carroll. His son, Henry Carroll, built the present house.

From the next owner, Henry Hill Carroll, the place was purchased by Edward Austen, at whose death it passed to his wife. She sold the property to J. Hall Pleasants in 1894. It was he who built the porches and the frame addition. In November, 1902, William H. Grafflin bought Clynmalira and owned it until 1910. Other owners included Mrs. Alfred L'Esperance, Mrs. Mary S. McGrath, and Mr. Clayton Pitts. The current owners, Dr. and Mrs. Thomas Rankin, purchased Clynmalira from Mrs. Rankin's father, Charles Yaeger. The Rankins have done extensive restoration and the mansion is in better condition than it has been for years.

The house is surrounded by huge shade trees and its yellow bricks gleam through the green tracery of the leaves. Clynmalira's most distinctive features are the inset porch with its great white columns running up two storeys to the arches just under the eaves and its facade. A second storey porch with a white balustrade lies behind the columns, creating a pleasing horizontal to the prevalent vertical lines. Huge chimneys and a complicated roof line add a quaint touch to such a large mansion.

The front door opens on the great hall, remarkable for its height. As there are no windows lighting it, the hall is dim and mysterious. Old portraits of the Carroll family by famous artists of a bygone day hang on the walls, with the impression of family and proud heritage impregnating the very air itself.

To the left of the hallway, and at right angles, is the stair hall with a graceful flight of steps reaching the upper storeys. In line with the front door is a large door opening on the porch and looking over the park-like grounds.

On the right of the main hall is the door to the living room. Next is the entrance to a sitting room. Across the hall is the door to the library which is ornamented by a great fireplace. The other two rooms have fireplaces also. The modern addition, built by J. Hall Pleasants, is on the left of the main house.

It is interesting to note that Clynmalira means "Sweet Air," the name borne by another property nearby, which also belonged to this same Carroll family.

HAMPTON

535 Hampton Lane, Towson

In all of Maryland, there is no more stately home than Hampton, one of the largest and most ornate mansions built during the post-Revolutionary War period. This great mansion is on Hampton Lane, off Dulaney Valley Road, just north of the Baltimore Beltway. The estate at one time comprised 24,000 acres, many of which are now under the waters of the Loch Raven Reservoir.

For 158 years, Hampton was the home of the Ridgely family, long prominent in Maryland. The original tract of 1500 acres was purchased in 1745. When iron ore deposits were found nearby, the Ridgelys expanded their land holdings and established the Northampton Ironworks, which supplied military supplies, including cannon and shot, to patriot forces during the Revolution. Hampton Mansion, built by Captain Charles Ridgely, was the result of profits made from the operation of the ironworks, land speculation following the Revolutionary War, and other agricultural and industrial interests.

The unique combination of classical design and five-part Georgian plan, developed on a grand scale, appears to have been formulated by Captain Ridgely and his chief carpenter, Jehu Howell. It was Howell, listed as "a very ingenious architect of Baltimore County" at his death in 1787, who suggested the use of the cupola which surmounts the roof like a royal crown. Though groundbreaking and initial masonry work was begun in 1783, the main house was not completed until 1790.

Captain Charles Ridgely married Rebecca Dorsey. Having no direct descendants at the time of his death, the Captain willed Hampton to his nephew, Charles Ridgely Carnan, with the proviso that he change his name to Charles Carnan Ridgely, as it was the Captain's strong desire to have a Ridgely in name as well as blood to own Hampton. Charles

Carnan Ridgely, who assumed Hampton in 1790, married Rebecca's sister, Priscilla Dorsey. He was active in politics, serving as a representative in the Maryland General Assembly from 1790 to 1795, a senator in that same legislative body from 1796 to 1800, and finally as Governor of Maryland from 1815 to 1818. After his death in 1829, succeeding generations of the Ridgely family continued to inhabit Hampton in a style commensurate with their social status.

Hampton remained in the Ridgely family until 1948, when it was acquired by the National Park Service. For 30 years, the Society for the Preservation of Maryland Antiquities administered Hampton as a historic site for the National Park Service. On October 1, 1979, the National Park Service took over full responsibility for the mansion, though a volunteer group, known as Historic Hampton, Inc., still operates the gift shop and offers volunteer aid to the property.

Known for their beauty and renown, the formal gardens and grounds of Hampton contribute to the grandeur of the estate. Notable trees on the grounds include red cedars, catalpas, magnolias and other native and exotic specimens. The spacious grounds contain many outbuildings including greenhouses, an ice house, stables and a restored orangerie. A recent land acquisition added significant buildings to the park, including the Lower House, slave quarters, the dairy and barns. Today, the furnishings of the mansion reflect the entire Ridgely residency. Hampton National Historic Site is open to the public, with free admission. The grounds are open daily from 9 a.m. to 5 p.m., except on January 1 and December 25. The Mansion itself is open daily from 11 a.m. to 5 p.m. and Sundays from 1 p.m. to 5 p.m., with guided tours given every half-hour, with the last tour beginning at 4:30 p.m.

THE PHILPOT HOUSE

13920 Mantua Mill Road, Glyndon

Half a mile from Deadman Run and not far from St. John's Church, on the side of a hill commanding a fine view, is the Philpot House, now the Green Spring Valley Hounds Club House. This old brick mansion is cradled in a grove of trees, with well-kept lawns before it, and a brick terrace in the rear. Nearby kennels house the hunt club hounds.

Bryan Philpot came from Stamford, England, reputedly with a special license from King George III to conduct business in Baltimore Town. Bryan Philpot, Jr., was born there is 1749, and was a soldier in the American Revolution. He married Elizabeth Johnson in 1796. On April 11, 1812, he died, leaving five children: Bryan, Mary Elizabeth, Clarissa, John, and Edward Pickering who was graduated from St. John's College in 1829. Two years later young Mr. Philpot married Sarah Merryman of Monkton, Maryland, who died in 1867. Eight years after her death he married Anna Merryman of Virginia. The property consisted of one hundred and ninety-five acres when the Philpot estate sold it in 1925 to the Green Spring Valley Hunt Club. Since then the house has been carefully restored, much of the old woodwork having been cleaned and polished.

From the front, the house appears to be the usual type of Colonial brick home built about 1780. It is two-and-a-half storeys high with three dormer windows and two brick chimneys. In the rear there is a charming little courtyard formed by the juncture of the large brick house and the smaller one-and-a-half storey older wing. The second floor windows of the main section overlooking this courtyard are rather unusual, as they contain twenty panes, twelve in the upper sash and only eight in the lower.

A small porch shades the front door which opens on a hall running through the house. The stairway, fitted together with wooden pins, as is all the woodwork in the house, is beautifully made. The slight irregularities of the balustrades together with the satin smoothness of the hand rail reveal the craftsmanship of the Colonial carpenter. On either side of the hall are doors to the parlor and dining room from which a modern kitchen is reached. Opening off the dining room, where there is a fine mantel similar to the one in the parlor, is the old wing. Here the bare beams still can be seen and the enormous brick fireplace, with the steps winding over it, harbors a great fire crane holding an ancient pot.

The whole building preserves admirably the atmosphere of Colonial days. When the hunt assembles on a cold autumn morning, the ladies in their black habits, the gentlemen in their pink, and the eager hounds might be the lively ghosts of a famous meet of the late eighteenth century. The sound of the horn sends the hunt away in orderly confusion, leaving the old house sleeping serenely on the hillside which it has graced so long.

HOMEWOOD

Charles and 34th Streets, Baltimore

Homewood, now part of the Johns Hopkins University Campus, first belonged to the illustrious Charles Carroll of Carrollton. Carroll, a signer of the Declaration of Independence, bought the "Merryman's Lott" tract in 1794 for his son, Charles. When Charles Carroll, Jr. married Harriet Chew of Philadelphia, the elder Carroll presented the land to the couple as a wedding present along with sufficient funds to build a suitable house.

Charles Carroll, Jr. directed the construction of Homewood. Carroll exceeded his father's generous estimate for construction, as he saw to it that the mansion was built according to his own good taste. Though the elder Carroll footed bills in excess of $30,000 for Homewood, the mansion was considered a "jewelbox" when it was finally completed in 1810. In 1824, Carroll bought the estate from his self-indulgent, recalcitrant son, whose wife had left him by that time with her father-in-law's blessings. Charles Carroll of Carrollton managed Homewood, which he considered "a most improvident waste," until his son died in 1825.

Ownership of Homewood then fell to Charles Carroll, son of Charles Carroll, Jr., grandson of Charles Carroll of Carrollton. Charles Carroll and wife Mary Diggs lived there until he inherited Doughoregan Manor from his grandfather in 1832. Charles Carroll's second son, John Lee Carroll, was born in Homewood in 1830 and later became Governor of Maryland. In 1839, Charles Carroll sold Homewood and 120 acres at public auction. Samuel Wyman, a successful Baltimore merchant, bought the property at that time for $25,150. Wyman lived in Homewood with his family until 1865.

When Samuel Wyman died in 1894, the Homewood estate was divided between his two sons. From 1897 to 1902 Homewood housed the Country School for Boys, now known as Gilman School. In 1902, Homewood was offered to the Johns Hopkins University as the site for a new campus. The architects constructing the Hopkins campus around Homewood repeated its traditional Federal motif in their design of the additional buildings. Beginning in 1916, the Homewood mansion served as the University Faculty Club, and from 1932 to 1936 it was a house museum. Since 1936, Homewood has been used for college administrative offices.

Homewood is a fine example of late Georgian or "Federal" style architecture. It is a symmetrical five-part Palladian country house in the pre-Revolutionary Maryland tradition. The house is similar to earlier houses such as Tulip Hill and Wye House—a five-part plan with large central block, small wing connected by a hyphen on each end, and the full height tetra-style portico.

Characterized by its refined, delicate, and sophisticated atmosphere, Homewood is replete with details. Wood carvings predominate. The cornice, the capitals of the columns, and the doorway pilasters are filled with miniature reeding, fluting, running 's', and acanthus leaves. The mansion also conveys an appearance of flatness, as the long, narrow windows are flush against the exterior wall. Above all the windows on the first floor are marble window sills and panels. The roof of the main block has two round head dormers with Gothic sash. The south side of each hyphen has a doorway with a semi-circular fanlight.

The fanlighted front door opens on a wide hall running through the house to the beautiful rear entrance with its fanlight of more delicate tracery. On the right side of the hall is the great drawing room. As in the dining room opposite it, the long, floor-to-ceiling windows allow maximum light to accent the elaborately carved interior. Behind the two front rooms is a narrow corridor separating them from the music room and the bedrooms. The two wings are approached by the usual hyphens which lead to the kitchen and library. Here the master of the house kept the records of his farming; for at the time Homewood was built, fields and virgin forest surrounded it and the town was quite a distance away.

MOUNT CLARE MANSION

Carroll Park, Baltimore

The origins of Mount Clare can be traced to the ambitions of a determined and brilliant young Irishman, Dr. Charles Carroll. Between 1715 when he arrived in the colonies from Ireland to 1755 when he died, Dr. Carroll amassed one of the six most considerable fortunes in the colony. His son, Charles Carroll the Barrister, inherited most of this wealth at the age of thirty-two, and in 1756 began to build a manor house on one of his father's land tracts, the "Georgia Plantation." It lay along the northern banks of the Middle Branch of the Patapsco River near Baltimore Town. Within four years Charles had completed the main block of the mansion. He called his great house Mount Clare after his sister, Mary Clare and his grandmother, Clare Dunn.

Today, the mansion is situated in Carroll Park in southwest Baltimore still high on its knoll amidst a grove of ancient English elms planted by Generals Washington and Lafayette and Charles Carroll over 200 years ago. Mount Clare is the oldest pre-revolutionary house in the vicinity of Baltimore and has great historical significance in terms of its builder and its location.

The Barrister, whose legal studies at the Middle Temple in London distinguished him from the three other Charles Carrolls living in Maryland at the time, has largely been forgotten in spite of the significant role he played in the founding of Maryland. He is often confused with a distant, younger relative, Charles Carroll of Carrollton, who was a signer of the Declaration of Independence. The Barrister was responsible in part for writing the Maryland Declaration of Rights and the State Constitution. Later, he was asked to be Chief Judge of Maryland, but had to decline because of chronic malaria.

Strategically well-placed near an important supply route during the revolution, Mount Clare hosted Generals Washington and Lafayette more than once. In fact, Washington became a close friend of the Carrolls, corresponding with Mrs. Carroll about her orangery and the one he hoped to build at Mount Vernon.

The mansion is a fine example of the English Baroque style adapted to mid-Georgian tidewater architecture. Most of the bricks for the mansion were made and fired on the property. Terraces of falls (still visible today) were planted in beautiful gardens and dropped sedately away from the house towards the river.

In 1817 when the Barrister's widow Margaret died there were no immediate heirs to the property. Mount Clare was bequeathed to Charles Carroll's nephew, James Maccubbin, on the condition that he legally assume the name Carroll. By 1850-51 the last of the Maccubbin Carrolls had moved out of the mansion. James Maccubbin Carroll, Jr. then leased Mount Clare as a hotel.

During the post-Carroll era the house saw a variety of uses. The West Baltimore Scheutzen (Shooting) Society leased the property and house in the 1870's and 1880's for use as a social club, shooting range and beer garden. Smaller buildings that had flanked the mansion to the east and west were demolished during this period, and a two story wing was added to the west end.

In 1890, as part of a city-wide beautification program, the Baltimore City Park Board bought the house and grounds for what is now Carroll Park. The present wings were constructed by the Park Board in 1908 to house restrooms for the park. They have now been remodeled to recreate an 18th-century library and kitchen.

In 1917 the Maryland Chapter of the Colonial Dames leased the house and began to restore it to its former elegance. The Colonial Dames now operate Mount Clare as an historical mansion. A remarkable number of original artifacts have been returned to the house, including portraits of the Barrister and Margaret Carroll by Charles Willson Peale. Fittingly, much of the furniture, silver and procelain that once had been acquired with care and taste by the Carrolls has been returned at last to Mount Clare, giving visitors an unparalled view of authentic 18th-century interiors.

SAINT PAUL'S RECTORY

24 West Saratoga Street, Baltimore

Saint Paul's the mother parish of Baltimore, was organized in 1692. The present Rectory, situated at 24 West Saratoga Street, at the head of Liberty Street on land given by John Eager Howard, is within one block of the busiest section of the commercial district of Baltimore. The house, built during the rectorship of the Reverend Dr. William West, was begun in 1789 and finished in 1791, but the devoted rector, who had gathered funds for it, died just before it was completed.

Rising high above the street on the original level of the soil, now supported by a six foot retaining wall, St. Paul's Rectory is a fine example of late eighteenth century architecture. The entire house is of brick laid in Flemish bond exhibiting the careful and precise craftmanship found in much colonial construction in Maryland and vicinity. The central section of two-and-a-half storeys with dormer windows is balanced by small wings on either side, both two-and-a-half storeys in height. A pediment under a fine Palladian window retaining some of the original glass interrupts the facade. Beneath this is the front door, reached by four stone steps.

The large hall runs through the house to the back, broken in its sweep by an oval arch which divides it into two sections. On the right is a large parlor with a very simple fireplace. Beyond the hall arch on the right is the door to the large dining room, containing beautiful period furniture and a plain mantel. On the right of the back hall is a reading room, small and cozy, with built-in bookcases flanking a mantel. A second door from the dining room leads to the pantry, kitchen and store rooms, added in 1906.

The most remarkable feature of St. Paul's Rectory is the main staircase. The wall at the end of the hall is octagonal and the steps follow the angles of the wall faithfully, winding without a landing to the second floor. Here there is a hall from which the stairs again ascend to the next floor. The only panelling in the house is at the foot of the stairway.

The first occupant of the house was the Reverend J.G.J. Bend, D.D., Rector from 1791 to 1812. He was succeeded by the (Right) Reverend James Kemp in 1812, who was Rector until 1827. After him came the Reverend William E. Wyatt, D.D., who lived in the Rectory from 1827 to 1864. The Reverend Milo Mahan, D.D., resided there from 1864 to 1870, and he was followed by the Reverend J.S.B. Hodges, who guided the parish from 1870 to 1905 and exerted a lasting influence in liturgy and music.

In October 1906, the Reverend Arthur B. Kinsolving, D.D., became Rector of the parish. In the summer of the same year, under the guidance of Douglas H. Thomas, Jr., architect, a number of new bathrooms were put in, and the kitchen and the laundry built in the rear, without altering the original lines of the house.

Following Dr. Kinsolving's retirement, the Reverend Harry Lee Doll, D.D., was called to be Rector in 1942 and occupied the house with his wife and three daughters. In 1955, Dr. Doll was elected Bishop Suffragan of the Diocese of Maryland and the following year was succeeded by the Very Reverend Frederick Ward Kates who came from the Deanship of the Cathedral of Saint John the Evangelist in Spokane, Washington. In 1961, the Reverend Halsey Moon Cook became Rector. He, his wife, and six children represented downtown Baltimore's most visible young family. After extensive renovation of the interior of the Rectory, the Reverend William Noble McKeachie became the fifteenth Rector of Saint Paul's Parish in 1981. With the birth of their first child, the McKeachies furnished the Palladian window room as a nursery once again.

Today St. Paul's Rectory is an enduring beacon to all who are made happy by the beauty and leisure of another age and is the oldest continuously occupied residence in the City of Baltimore.

COLD SATURDAY

Gamber Road, Finksburg

On the east side of Gamber Road, about a half mile south of Route 140, is a charming old stone house which bears the quaint title of Cold Saturday. Known for many years as Clover Hill, the original grant of two hundred and forty acres was patented as Cold Saturday in 1765. Architecture and construction methods suggest that the dwelling was probably built shortly after this.

Cold Saturday is on a ridge overlooking a charming valley and a lake which was made by damming up a small stream at the bottom of the hill. The front porch, which originally had massive columns rising two storeys, is now less ornate. The old one storey wing on the left has been raised to correspond with a proposed new wing on the right side. The house, with its three storey central section, is larger than are most early Carroll County homes.

The beautiful front door has a fanlight over it which is duplicated over the second floor window directly above this door. Large rooms to the right and left of the hall are wainscoted to three feet and all through the house there are chair rails. The stairway to the upper floors rises in a well off the left of the hall. The luxury suggested by fine marble mantel pieces and other details of decoration supports the tradition that Cold Saturday was the finest dwelling of its day in Carroll County.

Among the stories connected with the house is one concerning a boy who hanged himself in the attic. His ghost has been reported to have been heard moving about overhead; but the sounds always have been traced to flying squirrels.

In Colonial times the owners of the property were ardent horsemen and even went to the expense of importing grooms from England. The black farm hands were as much astonished by the experts as were the Cockneys at not being lodged among red Indians. In former days the meadows in front of the house were filled with jumps and hurdles, and the Green Spring Valley Hunt Club rode out by tally-ho to take part in hunts and horse shows.

The property has passed through many hands. It is recorded that Governor Thomas Swann bought Cold Saturday from Sir Algernon Tillard in 1888. He, in turn, conveyed it to James Gittings, in whose family it remained for the next twenty-eight years. Other prominent names connected with the land are Poultney, Cole, La Motte, Butler, Taylor, and Caples. The previous owners, Mr. and Mrs. H. Hamilton Hackney, were raising pure bred Aberdeen-Angus beef cattle. They took a great deal of pride in Cold Saturday and spared neither effort nor interest in making it worthy once more of its builder and those who since have cherished it. The farm is presently owned by Barbara and Erroll Houck, who raise thoroughbred horses for show and racing in the modern show barn which was built after fire destroyed the main barn.

THE ELMS

Finksburg

Two and a half miles west of Reisterstown and a short distance from Finksburg, there once stood a delightful home known as the Elms. In times gone by it was also called Beall's Venture and White Oak Bottom. Today nobody knows who Beall was and the elms are not remembered by the oldest inhabitants. The stage road which used to pass in front of the house was abandoned when the new Westminster Pike was built.

The Elms was erected about 1760, but the architect is not recorded, and a careful searching of the title and old deeds has failed to show to whom the original grant was made. However, it is known that Francis Scott Key, Jr., bought the house in 1835 and lived there until 1850.

In 1869, John J. Gray purchased the property from Mrs. Mercer, a niece of Johns Hopkins, and it remained in the Gray family for many years. At Mr. Gray's death it passed to his daughters and in 1939 was in the possession of Frances Ely Gray, who made her home there during the summer seasons.

The house was large, two-and-a-half storeys high with dormer windows and a small wing to the left. As is true of so many of the old homes in Maryland, the front became the back, caused in this case by the shift of the main road. Wide porches ran across two sides and gave shade in the summer heat. The stone foundation, quarried on the place, was two feet thick and provided a sturdy base for the brick walls.

The old front door was gained by a small porch with columns and its wide panels give on a commodious hall at the back of which are the stairs to the upper floors. On the right was the door to the reception room with its corner fireplace, and on the left was the entrance to the parlor, where the fireplace is immediately to the right of the door. A wide opening in the partition wall gave access to a smaller room behind. On the right of the hall was a room similar to the reception room, also with a corner fireplace.

In the room behind the parlor, on the left, were steps leading to the wing where the kitchen and dining room were located. In the small kitchen hall were the early American equivalent of room bells, each with a different tone, so that the room could be identified by sound. They were connected with every chamber in the house and substantiated the supposition that the Elms used to be an inn when stage coaches rolled down the Indian trail.

There is a tragic story reputed to be connected with one of the owners of the Elms, Robert Oliver, at that time living on his estate on the site of the present Greenmount Cemetery. Thinking that he had discovered a hated neighbor on his property, he shot the supposed invader. To his horror he discovered that he had killed his own daughter, who had dressed in her brother's clothes to meet her lover.

Near the Elms lived Madame Betsy Patterson Bonaparte, who often drove there with her little son in an ox cart from her home, Montrose, half a mile away.

The Elms was burned, blasted and bulldozed in 1954 to make way for the Liberty Reservoir, a sad fate for such a beautiful house. Its bricks were used to build another home.

THE SHRIVER HOUSE

3311 Littlestown Pike, Westminster

In Union Mills, 7 miles north of Westminster, on the right hand side of Littlestown Pike going north, stands one of the old brick mills from which the town receives its name. Almost in its shadow a quaint two storey Z-shaped frame building, large and rambling, quietly basks in the sun. Fine old shade trees and well kept lawns and gardens provide a fitting setting for a family rich in tradition and famous throughout Maryland. The Shriver House was erected by Andrew Shriver and his brother, David, Jr., but the latter disassociated himself from his brother and moved elsewhere.

The house shows the difference between the settling of the upper and lower counties. In 1797, Andrew and his brother built the first part of the dwelling of logs, which can be found today under the wide clapboards of the right wing. Carroll County was a wilderness and those who settled there were pioneers. Building materials and crude furniture were hewed and carved from the virgin forest. The Shriver House was pegged together, and the window frames are still joined by the original fastenings.

The dwelling is so rambling that it would be difficult to give a complete description of the interior here. The right leg of the Z has a great chimney of brick and stone. To this a few rooms were added about 1825, and then a further section, complicated by a wing, was constructed. There are porches all around the house. One two storey verandah in the rear looks as though it came straight from Charleston. The whole building is a series of delightful nooks and small unexpected rooms, up or down a few steps as the floor levels follow the unevenness of the site.

The Shriver family occupied their home for six generations. After the death of the first Andrew, his son Andrew K. Shriver inherited the property passing it on to his son Henry Wert and Louis E. Shriver. In turn they passed it on to Henry Wert's daughters Mrs. Thomas Kemp and Mrs. H.M.J. Klein. Mrs. Kemp died in 1958 and having no children, left the property to her three nephews Dr. Frederick S. Klein, Dr. Philip

S. Klein, and Richard Klein. The Klein brothers opened the home as a privately run museum until 1964 when the Union Mills Homestead Foundation was chartered. Today the Foundation continues to operate the Union Mills Homestead Museum for the Carroll County Commissioners.

The brick Grist Mill across the way from the house has been restored and is open to the public. It was built in 1797 and operated as a merchant mill until 1942. A large wooden water-wheel powers the mill stones to turn and grind corn meal. Although the grist mill went through many changes over the years, it has been reconstructed to the 1830's with all wooden gears.

It is related that Audubon, the great naturalist, first reported the oriole in the neighborhood while staying at the Shriver home. During the War Between the States, on June 30, 1863, General Barnes, with his brigade of the Fifth Corps of the Federal Army, spent the night there. He was just too late to catch General Jeb Stuart of the Confederate Army, who had stopped there the previous night.

In the Shriver House, over the entrance hall, is a room which is named after Washington Irving, as the famous author slept there. This is shown in the etching, which was done from the second storey of the nearby mill. Although it is reported that Irving confidently expected to see ghosts in such an old dwelling, he must have reckoned without Rattlesnake Hill, which is a mile away. No self respecting spirit could afford to live anywhere in this locality but on the slopes of that hill. Consequently there are no stories of Headless Horsemen to be found in Union Mills, but any resident of the town can tell hair-raising tales of the ectoplasmic inhabitants of the haunted Rattlesnake Hill.

The Union Mills Homestead is open from Tuesday through Sunday in June, July and August and on weekends in May and September. Each year there are three special events, the Flower and Plant Market, the Old Fashioned Corn Roast, and the Poinsettia and Greens Sale.

BELMONT

off Elibank Drive, Elkridge

Ten miles west of Baltimore in the highlands of the beautiful Patapsco River, with a sweeping view of twenty miles of rolling country, is Belmont, built by Caleb Dorsey of Annapolis in 1738. Here he and his charming bride, Priscilla Hill of West River, lived to a ripe old age, and were frequently visited by his father, also Caleb Dorsey, who lived at Hockley-in-ye-Hole.

The house, crowning the top of a hill, is long and narrow, being for the most part but one room deep. The situation was selected by its picturesque surveyor, Mordecai Moore, who had laid out ten thousand acres for himself in the Patapsco section in 1730, calling the property "Moore's Morning Choice". However, he never was able to realize his dream of building a home there, as he was forced by adverse circumstances to sell the location to Caleb Dorsey, the Elder, in 1735.

The road to Belmont is long and winds through wooden glens, offering glimpses of pastoral scenes much the same today as they were in the early eighteenth century. A circular driveway approaches the small porch, from which the front door opens into a hall panelled to the ceiling. On the left is the entrance to the drawing room, from which the library is reached. Beyond the library is the great sunny ballroom with a large fireplace. This room has rounded corners, making it more intimate.

Opening from the drawing room is a comfortable sitting room. Although all the front rooms are on a line, they are on different levels as the house follows the slope of the hill on which it is erected. Panelling is plentiful and carefully fitted. There are many evidences of superior hand craftsmanship.

For many generations the Dorsey family held Belmont. When its builder died, his oldest son, Edward Dorsey, inherited the property. Edward Dorsey was known to his neighbors as "Iron-Head Ned", and was renowned for the good iron he made, and for his obstinacy.

His daughter, Priscilla, also had a mind of her own, and, when consent was refused for her choice of Alexander Contee Hanson as a husband, she ran away. The groom had provided for every emergency. When their coach lost a cotter pin he had another handy and quickly replaced it, and the happy couple reached the minister in time to be married. Their son, Charles Grosvenor Hanson, married Anne Maria Worthington. They had five children.

In 1918 Belmont was purchased by Howard Bruce, whose wife was a lineal descendant of Caleb and Priscilla Dorsey. The Bruces lived at Belmont for 50 years and maintained and enlarged the old house in the true Colonial manner. Mr. and Mrs. Bruce and their children rode to hounds and took great interest in point-to-point racing. Numbered among their hunters was the internationally known Billy Barton.

The property was purchased in 1961 by Ambassador David K.E. Bruce, cousin of Howard Bruce, breaking the direct lineal succession. After three years, the Ambassador presented the estate to the Smithsonian Institution. The Smithsonian operated Belmont as a conference center until 1983, when the conference center was acquired by the American Chemical Society, which continues the same tradition of excellent hospitality to world leaders in science, art and industry.

BURLEIGH MANOR

Old Centennial Lane, Ellicott City

Adjoining Doughoregan Manor is an estate on which stands a fine old turn-of-the-century home known as Burleigh Manor. This beautiful house lies on the top of a hill five miles from Ellicott City just off Centennial Lane, in the midst of rolling country, and commands an extensive view of the surrounding terrain. Today the property consists of about four hundred acres, about two hundred of which are fine farm land. The original plot was two thousand three hundred forty-five acres.

The brick mansion was built by Colonel Rezin Hammond about 1800 for his nephew, Denton Hammond. Colonel Hammond, brother of Mathias Hammond, was a bachelor and delighted in spending his time and money on the favored son of his brother. Here Denton Hammond and his bride, Sarah Hall Baldwin, lived many years until their death. Their son, Colonel Mathias Hammond, inherited the property. He married Mary Hanson and they had no sons, but the Hammond name was kept in the family when one of their two daughters, Grace Hammond, married Richard Creigh Hammond, a cousin. "Miss Grace" Hammond lived at Burleigh Manor for many years until she died in 1928 at an advanced age.

Charles McAlpin Pyle, of New York, bought the property in 1935 from Mrs. Hammond's heirs. At this time the house was not in the best of repair and a great deal of careful restoring and rebuilding, particularly on the interior, was required to make Burleigh Manor into one of the most beautiful homes in Howard County. Bathrooms had to be cunningly hidden under stairs and cupboards created in rooms without destroying the symmetry of the design. The great fireplace was kept in the hunting room, which was panelled in raw pine wood; the old kitchen has been modernized.

Burleigh Manor was then purchased by Angier Biddle Duke of Philadelphia, as a home for his daughter and her husband. It was then purchased by St. Timothy's School, which soon sold it to the Iverson family. They did a thorough restoration. After the deaths of the elder Iversons, it was purchased by the Burleigh Manor Partnership. One of the partners, Samuel Rose, and his wife are now making Burleigh Manor their home, after extensive restoration work and a six year period of vacancy.

The building is unusual in that it seems unfinished, for the plan is that of a central section with flanking wings, of which there is only one. At first sight this disproportion is disturbing, but soon the inherent charm of the house asserts itself and the apparently jarring note is recognized as just another of the quaint conceits of the Colonial architect, who occasionally could be as cunning in his dissonances as any modern composer.

A tree lined avenue leads up the circular drive before the front door. An elliptical headed doorway with a leaded fanlight and side-lights opens into the great hall. The rear entrance follows the design of the front door and an arch, spanning the hall, is also elliptical. At right angles to the hall on the left is the stairway with graceful low rises and broad treads.

The drawing room is on the immediate left of the entrance with the door to the dining room opposite. Farther down the hall on the right is the entrance to the sitting room. All these rooms have large beautifully carved mantels. The partitions are all of brick. The kitchen and servants' wing is reached through a passage.

It is impossible to convey in print the quiet beauty that surrounds Burleigh Manor. Many of the great homes of Maryland seem to flaunt their glory, but Burleigh Manor steals into the heart like the amen at the end of a simple hymn.

CHERRY GROVE

2937 Jennings Chapel Road, Woodbine

In 1766 the land on which Cherry Grove stands was granted to Captain Benjamin Warfield. He finished the house two years later. It remained in the Warfield family for 6 generations until 1939 when it was purchased by Arthur G. Nichols, Jr., the present owner.

Benjamin Warfield received his title of Captain when he was commissioned by the Council on Monday, March 2, 1778, in the Elk Ridge Battalion of Militia. He had four sons. The oldest, Benjamin, died while a young man. Beale and Philemon Dorsey Warfield took part in the war of 1812, during which their father died. He left Cherry Grove to his youngest son, Joshua.

On February 26, 1817, Albert G. Warfield, named after Albert Gallatin, the first Secretary of the Treasury, was born in the old homestead. It was he who built the first section of what became the nearby Warfield mansion, Oakdale. Two of his six sons served in the Confederate Army, Gassaway Watkins Warfield dying at Camp Chase, Ohio, in 1864. His second son, Albert G. Warfield, Jr., became a well known civil engineer and served as a member of the American Scientific Commission to Japan in 1873. Edwin Warfield, son of Albert, became Governor of Maryland. His grandson sold the Oakdale mansion, but still resides in another home he built on the property he retained.

The house is on Jennings Chapel Road, formerly known as Rolling Road, two miles from Lisbon on the Frederick Road. Its quaint flat-roofed dormer windows look out over rolling country toward the rising sun. Only one-and-a-half storeys high, with a hipped roof, an uneven roof line and three brick chimneys thrusting their way to the sky, Cherry Grove is a fine example of an early settler's home. The house was built in sections, as there are three staircases and three front doors. Two of the sections were completed in 1768, and the third section was added in 1860, just prior to the Civil War. In 1907, the smaller of the original sections was torn down and fully rebuilt.

The front doors open into the three parts of the house. The central section, dating back to 1768, is divided into two rooms by panelling of stained wood to the ceiling. In the front room heavy beams, rudely channelled by hand, run across the ceiling and into the next room. The closely fitted boards of the second storey floor can be seen between these supports. To the left is the narrow staircase turning above the huge brick chimney, so large that the same flue serves a second fireplace in the rear room.

Over this fireplace is a plain mantel and beside it a door opening into the room to the right. This room had an outside doorway and a fireplace in the left corner with a small staircase squeezed between it and the wall. The right wing was at one time the kitchen with a separate fireplace.

There are three porches, one in front covering the first two sections of the house, one at the kitchen door which opens on the side, and one in the rear. All the windows and doors of the dwelling are rather small. Much of the old world charm of Cherry Grove is due to the hoary shingled roof, which has a patina like old bronze.

Although the cherry orchard from which the house took its name is gone there are magnificent old trees which provide shade in summer and shelter in winter.

DOUGHOREGAN MANOR

Manor Lane, Ellicott City

One mile from the Baltimore-Frederick Pike and five miles west of Ellicott City is Doughoregan Manor, early dwelling of the Carrolls of Carrollton. This famous old home is not matched by any other Colonial mansion in the state of Maryland, either in magnificence or historical background. The mere fact that it was the seat of Charles Carroll of Carrollton would insure its being of more than average importance, but the many famous men that frequented its halls have placed an aura of legend about the building.

It is difficult to visualize the style of living enjoyed by the man who was reputed to be the wealthiest American to side with the Colonies against England. The laundry alone that serviced the great home mansion is sixty feet long and three storeys high. Near it a large house for the manager of the estate is flanked by cabins for the slaves.

The first Charles Carroll, known as "the immigrant," came to Maryland in 1688. To him were granted sixty thousand acres to compensate for property in Ireland lost in the Civil Wars. Later he acquired fifteen thousand acres in Howard County, where he built Doughoregan Manor, completed in 1717. He was followed by his son, Charles Carroll of Annapolis, whose son was the Signer, Charles Carroll of Carrollton. This brightest star in the Carroll constellation took up his residence in the manor house in 1765, and lived there until 1832, last survivor of the signers of the Declaration of Independence.

Charles Carroll of Carrollton outlived his son, known as Charles Carroll of Homewood, and it was his grandson, Charles Carroll, called "the Colonel", to whom were bequeathed his grandfather's broad acres.

His heir was his son, Charles Carroll, great grandson of the Signer, who married Caroline Thompson of Virginia. As they preferred to live abroad, the estate was sold to a brother, John Lee Carroll, Governor of Maryland, in 1875. The Governor's first wife was Anita Phelps of New York; his second was Mary Carter Thompson, sister of his brother's wife. His son by his first wife was also Charles Carroll, who left the property to the last Charles Carroll to own Doughoregan Manor. He sold to his uncle, Philip Acosta Carroll, whose son, Philip Carroll, now resides there. Thus it is that this property has been in the same family since it was granted.

The house, of yellow painted brick, is long and narrow, with two storeys, relieved by a wooden battlemented tower. The front door is in the center of the house, shaded by a small porch. At either end of the edifice are wings, the one on the left housing the servants. On the right is the chapel, where the Carroll family has held mass under the tall rounded narrow stained glass windows every Sunday since the altar was consecrated. It is here that the body of Charles Carroll of Carrollton is buried. His spirit hovers so strongly about the home which he loved, that even those who come upon Doughoregan Manor in ignorance of its history cannot help but be impressed by the atmosphere of dignity and beauty which enfolds the greatest Colonial manor of Maryland.

BON AIR

off Laurel Brook Road, Fallston

If Medical Hall is like a French town house, Bon Air is its opposite, a rustic chateau. Situated near Gunpowder Falls, and almost adjoining the old Meeting House in Fallston, this two-and-a-half storey dwelling seems to have been lifted bodily from the banks of the Aix River and transported to Harford County.

The plan is like a Capital L; the large central section has a left wing with an additional wing at right angles. The final plan of such a building would be a courtyard, enclosed on three sides, with a grill work fence and huge gates across the open end.

The French features of this house are the plan, the curved hip roof, and the curved mantels. One has only to remember that the builder was Colonel C.F.F. de la Porte, Colonel en Second of the Vennois Regiment, to realize that this Gallic influence was not attained by chance.

Colonel de la Porte came from France and settled in Santo Domingo, whence he was driven by the black revolt in 1794. He brought with him his family and apparently great wealth. His free display of this wealth gave rise to rumors that he was a pirate. For many years holes appeared in the fields near Bon Air where some hopeful treasure seekers had plied their midnight shovels.

When the Colonel died, Betsy Herbert de la Porte inherited the property in 1803, and twenty-one years later the brother of the Colonel, Francis de la Porte, became the owner. The Colonel, his wife, Betsy, and his brother were buried in the arched tomb situated to the rear of the house.

The last de la Porte to own Bon Air was Pierre Louis August Marchand, a nephew of Francis. He inherited the land in 1827, only to sell it to Francis Gallega four years later. From his it was acquired by Caleb Harman, from whose possession it passed to Benjamin Ferris of Wilmington, Delaware. In 1858 the little chateau came into the hands of James T. Watson. It is now owned by C. John and Barbara McCann Sullivan.

The stairway to the second floor rises in the hallway. It is made without the use of nails, each part being doweled to the next section. According to an old picture, the wing immediately next to the house originally had but one-and-a-half storeys with dormer windows. It was raised to a full two storeys during the 1830's.

The heavy bracing of the mansard roof and four strong hooks on the ceiling of the second floor lend a touch of veri-similitude to the story that Colonel de la Porte, who was a sea captain as well as in the army under Rochambeau, had become so used to a hammock that he refused to sleep in anything else.

MEDICAL HALL

Medical Hall Road, Bel Air

Medical Hall lies in a little valley some seven miles from the center of Bel Air, and near the town of Churchville in Harford County. It is famous as having been the home of Dr. John Archer, who received from the University of Pennsylvania, June 21, 1768, the first medical degree awarded in America.

The mansion is two-and-a-half storeys high with dormer windows, and is made to seem much taller because of a high basement and the steps leading up to the four columns of the pedimented porch. This house has many architectural features in common with De La Brooke in St. Mary's County. The foundations are of stone. The brick building is covered with stucco, with a slate roof and a large brick chimney at either end. The dormers are well designed with a broken pediment and two attached columns flanking a curved-top window with twelve panes.

On entering the front door, placed in the exact center of the facade, the eye is immediately taken with the design of the beautiful old French wallpaper which covers the hall walls. This is a representation of the taking of the Bastille, depicted with force and clarity.

The hall runs through the house to the rear porch. On the right is the entrance to the reception room with its individual fireplace. Through a wide door we see the sitting room, also heated by a fireplace. All the mantels are different in design and finely carved. On the other side of the hall is the door to a room similar to the reception room, and in the back is the dining room. In the houses of this type the kitchen was in the basement, and food was carried up on a dumb-waiter. It

was an arrangement which attained much popularity on the Continent and in the great English mansions of the late eighteenth century.

The stairway is exceptionally fine. It rises on the left of the hall just beyond the door to the sitting room. Mahogany stairs are guarded by thin, elegant balustrades. The banister is carefully curved and rounded and curls about at the bottom. Nowhere in the house is there any panelling or even a chair rail.

Medical Hall, hiding behind its white wooden gates, is much like the type of house to be seen in the suburbs of Paris. It looks a little out of place in the rolling hills of Harford County, making the bewildered observer listen vainly for the honk of a French taxi.

It is related that Dr. Archer built the house as the result of a dream in which he saw his mother's home demolished by fire. So stirred was he that he immediately undertook the construction of Medical Hall, close by, and moved in as soon as it was finished. He also conducted a medical school there during the 1780's and 1790's, the first school of continuing education for practicing physicians.

Dr. Archer had six sons, from the last of whom, Judge Stevenson Archer, are descended many of the great names of the county. From 1943 to 1981, the Sidney Hall family resided at Medical Hall. In 1982, the property was acquired by Dr. Sidney D. Kreider, a member of the faculty of the Johns Hopkins School of Medicine. Dr. Kreider has uncovered the foundation of Dr. Archer's medical office and is planning its restoration.

SION HILL

Level Road, Havre de Grace

Sion Hill is inland a few miles from the Susquehanna River and about the same distance from Havre de Grace. It is a well proportioned, elegant house of brick, obviously the home of gentlefolk ever since it was built in 1775 by the Rev. John Ireland from England. He started a school there but when this was not successful he sold the property to Gideon Dennison.

This Revolutionary period home is one of the finest of its type in Maryland. It is a large two storey house with a central portion, and flanking wings of one-and-a-half storeys. The wings are wedded to the main structure by a sloping flat roof pitched against the walls of the central building. It was in the right wing that the school was held for some time.

The enormously wide chimneys, one at either end of the main part of the house, soar into the clear air. Above the garden porch is a fine Palladian window over which is a formal design often found in the detail of Georgian decoration. Above this window is a beautiful semi-circular tracery light illuminating a commodious attic. The roof, with its pedimental formation, has an exceptionally fine frieze of dentils. Such is the perfection of the house that one wonders if John Ireland, the designer, had not also been a student of architecture.

The present entrance is the former rear door, opening on a hall running the depth of the house. On the right is the entrance to the parlor, then the stairwell, followed by a door to the drawing room. On the left are the entrances to the large dining room and the study. An arch spans the hall, interrupting the plain heavy moulding.

When Minerva Dennison, daughter of Gideon Dennison, married Commodore John Rodgers, senior officer of the United States Navy, she brought Sion Hill to him as her dowry. Commodore Rodgers commanded both the *Constitution* and the *North Carolina.* The house has been in the Rodgers family ever since. From its walls have gone forth heroes of both services, particularly the Navy. Colonel Robert S. Rodgers, next owner of the mansion, took a conspicuous part in the Navy's peaceful penetration of Japan, in 1852, and married Sarah, eldest daughter of Commodore Matthew C. Perry. Consequently the house is full of Japanese and Korean trophies. Mrs. John A. Rodgers inherited Sion Hill from her husband, Rear-Admiral John A. Rodgers. Commander John Rodgers, hero of the first flight to Hawaii, was born here. Mrs. Rodgers survived her three sons, and upon her death, Sion Hill passed into the Meigs family, cousins of the Rodgers.

The house is now owned by Mrs. and Mrs. Montgomery Meigs Green, great great grandson of Commodore John Rodgers, who have lived there since 1946.

This Maryland home, steeped in the traditions of the past, stands proudly among the trees, as if aware that no shirker has ever called it home.

SOPHIA'S DAIRY

Route 40, Belcamp

On a branch of the Bush River two miles from Abington is Sophia's Dairy. The services of five redemptioners, who received their freedom when the building was finished, helped Aquilla Hall to build the house in 1768. In 1750 he married his first cousin, Sophia, after whom the home was named. She was the daughter of Colonel Thomas White.

Sophia's Dairy faces the river which lies a mile and a half away. It is of brick with a stone foundation sixty-four by forty-five feet, and is two storeys high with a large unfinished attic. The cellar has but one door, inside, under the stairs. To the right, and attached to the building, is a three room structure which can be entered directly from the house. This was formerly used as servants' quarters. Some distance from the house are the foundations of a large stable.

The plan of Sophia's Dairy is rectangular with two chimneys, supported by great arches in the cellar, rising through the ridge pole a quarter of the way from the ends of the house. On the first floor are two fireplaces back to back to each chimney. The front door is gained by a flight of steps to the pedimented porch. The exterior of the house is very plain, but the interior fully atones for it. Immediately the threshold is crossed a hall of surpassing loveliness, sixteen and a half feet wide and panelled to the chair rail, meets the eye. It runs to the rear door where another porch leads to an abandoned garden.

On the right of the hall are doors opening into a large dining room and the living room. On the left rises the crowning glory of Sophia's Dairy, the elaborate double Chinese Chippendale staircase, one of the finest in the state. Two flights of eleven steps meet at a landing, from which a single flight of four steps leads to a second landing. Here the stairs divide and in four more steps reach the second floor hall. The spindles, three to a step, and the hand rail, show the careful work of artists, as does the scroll on the step-ends. A panelled hand rail and panelling under the stairs complete the luxurious staircase.

The windows in all the rooms are deeply recessed and have twelve panes. In the dining room there is the same type of panelling as in the hall except for the mantel side which faces toward the front of the house. Here the panelling runs to the ceiling. On the left of the fireplace is a semi-circular cupboard built into the wall, and to the right, a short passageway to the kitchen. In this passage is the door to the annex and, facing it, a secret staircase just sixteen inches wide leading to a cupboard on the second floor.

Many a night messenger must have climbed this stairway to gain the second storey without the knowledge of the rest of the household; for Aquilla Hall was chairman of the group which wrote the Bush Declaration of Independence, signed March 22, 1775, one of the first documents of its kind in America.

Sophia's Dairy is now the property of the Bata Shoe Company, headquartered in Toronto, Canada.

BOHEMIA

4920 Augustine-Herman Highway, Earleville

Bohemia stands on a slight eminence by the south shore of the Bohemia River, opposite the junction of its two branches. The original grant was made in 1695 to Hugh McGregory of Cecil County. His son, Joseph, sold the land, then called "McGregory's Delight", in 1740, to Colonel John Baldwin. According to the approximate date of 1745, set as the building time, the present house was erected by this gentleman. He deeded it to his daughter, Catherine, who married George Milligan, of Chestertown.

For many years the place was called Milligan Hall, but this name was discarded about 1772 for the present Bohemia. Robert, son of George Milligan, died in 1806, and his son, George B. Milligan, inherited. Mary Catherine Milligan, wife of Louis McLane of Wilmington, Delaware, and sister of George, bought the land from her brother in 1828. In 1860 the property was broken up, and William Knight of Cecil County purchased the greater part of it and in 1866 passed it to his son, who died in 1910. At this time Catherine Milligan McLane bought the house and the immediate grounds which her grandmother had owned eighty years earlier. When Miss McLane died in 1927, she left Bohemia to her nephew, D.K. Este Fisher, Jr., who sold it to J.D. Otley, from whom it was purchased by the present owners. Since 1959, Mr. and Mrs. W. Harrison Mechling have made Bohemia their home.

The house, which stands in the midst of a grove of fine old trees, is a large two storey brick mansion with all-headed bond sunken in large panels on the land side. Two square chimneys rise through the roof line forming an interesting composition with the pedimented facade. The house originally had barns, stables, and other farm buildings. There was also a fine garden but that, like the outbuildings, is no more although the grounds are very beautiful. More than two hundred boxwood bushes complement the magnificent trees.

Of interest is the fact that the East wing, now covered with white clapboards, was originally of brick like the main body of the house. A number of years ago, Mr. du Pont purchased these old bricks for a restoration project at Winterthur. But Bohemia still has it quota. It has been estimated that there is the equivalent of two carloads of bricks in the chimneys which rise from the ten fireplaces in the house.

In contrast to the rather plain exterior is the richly decorated interior. The south door opens into a square hall with a remarkable Chinese Chippendale staircase ascending on the right. A door opening into the drawing room is in line with the front door, to the right and left of which are entrances into the music room and dining room. A beautiful plaster cornice and an exquisitely designed floral motif decorate the ceiling. In the drawing room a door on the left leads to a small room which has a corner fireplace; on the right is the entrance to a study.

In the music room there are designs in plaster on the ceiling and a very fine carved mantel with a broken pediment in the best Baroque style. The wall is embellished with plaster panel moulds and modeled ornaments above a chair rail. The dining room, wainscoted in blue flat boards three feet high, has a simply moulded mantel with panelling above it and on the left an inset cupboard with butterfly shelves and carving on the inside. To the right of the fireplace is the door into the study which has a cross vaulted plaster ceiling very unusual in Colonial houses. Between this room and the drawing room there once was a small stairway to the attic, built in the thickness of the chimney, and known as the "slaves' stairway."

The wainscotted drawing room is the largest in the house and has a carved and panelled mantel and chimney breast, as fine as any in Maryland. Quietly charming with subtle delights for the eye in every room, Bohemia testifies that its builder, Colonel John Baldwin, must have had irreproachable taste and a feeling for beauty.

OCTORARA

Rowlandsville Road, Conowingo

A half mile above Conowingo Dam, high up on the ridge along the Susquehanna Valley, stands Octorara. The grounds about the mansion slope towards Octorara Creek and the Susquehanna River. It is known that a large Indian fort was located nearby. This ancient seat of the Hall family was granted with one thousand acres to Richard Hall in 1640, by Lord Baltimore. The original house, of which but four rooms and attic remain, was built in 1690 as a summer place, not designed to survive the rigors of winter. The newer and larger section was added by Dr. Philip Syng Physick of Philadelphia between 1823 and 1828. Today it is a two-and-a-half storey brick house with dormer windows.

The front door opens into a hall with a bull's-eye window. On the left to the rear the stairs rise to the upper storeys. On the right of the hall a door opens into a commodious living room, with another large sitting room on the left. Between the rooms are folding doors, which permit the whole to be thrown into a ballroom. These rooms and the hall have solid wooden panelled shutters. A door from the hall leads into the library. From this point a few steps descend into what is left of the old house. A charming dining room, opening onto a two-storey porch, finally leads into a small wing added in 1835 when the family increased in number. At the very end of the house is the main kitchen. Near the five room tenant house is the Hall burial ground.

Smooth green lawns studded with great shade trees, and a colorful garden, form an appropriate setting for Octorara. There have been other names applied to the house, among them Mount Welcome, Mount Independence, and Hall's Lot. Mount Independence was the name given the mansion when General Lafayette was the guest of Colonel Hall there in 1781, before he and his army crossed the Susquehanna. The next night he spent at Rigbie Hall on the other side of the river on their way to York.

Colonel Richard Hall, last of the Hall family to own Octorara, was impoverished by the Revolution, and an uncle of Dr. Physick acquired the property. From him it went to Dr. Physick and then to Mrs. David Connor, his daughter. Her husband was a Commodore of the American Navy in the Mexican War. From her it descended to Philip Syng Connor, and then to his daughter, Mrs. P.S. Hale. Mrs. Phyllis Reeve O'Connor lived at and lovingly cared for Octorara for 23 years, before selling it in 1983 to Mrs. & Mrs. T. Jacques R. duPont, who are giving it a complete and beautiful restoration.

The Susquehannas, who frequented the neighborhood of Octorara and named the river, were regarded as the most ferocious of all the Eastern Indian tribes. They were the tallest and strongest Indians in America and many were known to have reached a height of seven feet. Today not a single member of that once mighty nation remains. They fought with neighboring tribes and settlers and among themselves, finally becoming extinct through their blind valor and bloodthirstiness. It seems strange that Octorara still stands while the great Susquehanna nation no longer exists.

OLDFIELD'S POINT

Oldfield's Point Road, Elkton

On the Elk River at Piney Creek Cove is Oldfield's Point. This is six miles from Northeast and almost nine miles from the center of Elkton. The house bearing the same name is located on a hill in parklike surroundings where numbers of small cedars and a few clumps of boxwood tell of the ancient garden. Towering trees grow close to the building. Nearby is a development of modern dwellings, which has taken Oldfield's as its name.

The land was originally part of St. John's Manor. It was first patented to John Pate of Virginia by Cecil Calvert in August of 1664. It was later granted to Captain John Kerr in April of 1675. About 1680, a portion was purchased by George Oldfield, who played an important part in the early history of Cecil County. In 1684, he was commissioned as a county attorney for Lord Baltimore and is believed to be the first State's Attorney of Cecil County. In a codicil to his will, Augustine Herman mentioned George Oldfield as a "trustworthy friend and neighbor" and appointed him as trustee of his estate.

The original dwelling was erected in 1768 by Captain John Ford, but it was burned by General Howe and his army when they were on their way to Philadelphia. When Captain Ford returned to his home to rebuild it, he found that the thick walls were in such good condition that they could be used again. The Colonists constructed their houses to last, as is shown at Cherryfield in Charles County, which was burned in 1835 and rebuilt with the same walls. On the eastern end of the house a slab of slate gives the date 1768 and the name of the builder.

The dwelling, two-and-a-half storeys high with dormer windows, is rather narrow for its length and height. A large cellar runs under the house. It may have been a thirst for the wine the Revolutionists kept there that led the English general to drop in so rudely on Captain Ford. The roof is shingled, and a broad verandah with slender wooden columns shades the land side of the house. The large one storey kitchen on the left was added at a later date. It has an enormous fireplace and a back door with a flight of steps to the hill outside.

The front door leads into a hall that is divided half-way down by an arch, beyond which, on the right, the wide staircase climbs to the upper storeys. In the front of the hall on the left is the entrance to the reception room. A door on the same side of the hall opens into the sitting room. Here there is a chair rail and the only wainscoting in the house. In the right far corner is a fireplace with a simple moulding and a very plain mantel. A similar arrangement is in the left far corner of the reception room.

Across the hall and opposite the door to the reception room, is the entrance to the dining room with its corner fireplace on the right. From this room a door leads to the kitchen. Another room corresponding to the sitting room lies behind the dining room.

For many years, the property was owned by Dr. G. Harlan Wells of Philadelphia. It is now owned by Dr. John Duckett, who also hails from Philadelphia.

GODLINGTON MANOR

Wilkins Lane, Chestertown

Overlooking the Chester River, approximately three miles south of Chestertown, stands Godlington Manor, a small two-storey clapboard house, now its original red, with a shingled gambrel roof, three chimneys, and long porches on both sides. One of the older buildings in Kent County, Godlington Manor's first structure was constructed in the late 17th century.

Godlington Manor was granted by King Charles II to a British merchant named Thomas Godlington in 1659 in return for his commitment to populate the property and put it into agricultural production. Godlington's grant stipulated that he must transport twenty persons to America and settle them on the property within a period of four years. Godlington, however, never fulfilled his obligation to colonize, and the property was eventually passed on to a Kent County official named Michael Miller in 1686. Miller became the first legal owner of Godlington, and was most likely the first owner to set foot on the property. Miller, who held many public offices, was one of the most powerful and prominent men in Kent County during the latter part of the seventeenth century.

The eastern-most portion of this Manor House was built during Michael's or his son Arthur's ownership. At that time, it was a long and arduous task to clear trees by hand; converting a piece of wilderness into a farm took years. Structures erected then were strictly utilitarian. Hence, the earliest part of the Manor House, a rectangle, consisted only of a sleeping loft above and a single room with a hearthed fireplace below.

The dwelling now has two sections, in one of which, only one-and-a-half storeys high, is the kitchen and pantry. In the large square kitchen there is a great stepped fireplace. On the left of this a ladder leads to the pitched attic, originally slave quarters. Through the large door you can see the original smoke house, the original milkhouse, and fifty yards beyond that, the Chester River.

The larger section of the home is shaded front and back by porches. The windows are few and small. The first architect had to consider the cost of glass and the number of openings to be defended in case of attack when he designed the building.

The dining room of Godlington Manor has a corner staircase on the left side of the fireplace. This fireplace wall is panelled to the low ceiling, only nine feet two inches in height. A cupboard on the left between the fireplace and steps is balanced on the right by the door to the kitchen. In the center of the opposite wall, facing the mantel, is the inside entrance to the living room. On the right of its fireplace, there is another closet and a corner staircase, enclosed as is the one in the drawing room. A large china closet with glass doors is on the left. This side of the room is panelled to the ceiling and a chair rail runs along the other three walls.

The most distinguishing feature of Godlington Manor is its decorative wall stenciling, a hand-painted forerunner of wallpaper. This stenciling is the only wall design of its kind found on the Delmarva Peninsula. The stenciling and wood graining have been restored to their late eighteenth century condition.

Descendants of Michael Miller have owned Godlington Manor for three centuries. Today, the estate is owned and leased by the Hiram S. Brown Trust. Brown, a graduate of Washington College, bought the farm around 1925 from a double-first cousin. Godlington Manor is open to the public twelve times a year. It has been completely restored to its 1840 appearance. Godlington sits at the end of a mile-long driveway, which is lined with alternating pine and dogwood trees. This Manor House is the result of a century of refinements, yet the concealed hand-hewn exterior timbers and other features of the house attest to its honest beginnings.

HINCHINGHAM

Route 445, Rock Hall

One of Kent County's finest showplaces is Hinchingham, located on the shore of the Chesapeake. This well-preserved brick mansion is a two-and-a-half storey building with a one-and-a-half storey brick wing to the north. Built in 1774, Hinchingham is one of the larger and more elegant residences constructed during that time in Kent County.

Hinchingham's history actually began in 1659 when Thomas Hynson was granted 2200 acres of land. By the mid-eighteenth century, this huge parcel of land had been divided up into nine smaller parcels. The largest of those, containing 700 acres, belonged to William Frisby, who served Kent County in several capacities including that of representative to the Maryland Assembly. Frisby, as the oldest son, had inherited the land from his father, who had died intestate in 1738. William Frisby then deeded 200 acres of land to his brother, James, "in consideration of the natural love and affection" that he felt for him. It was during the sixty years that James owned the property that the house called Hinchingham was erected.

James Frisby was a Commissioner and Justice in Kent County in the 1760's. Married four times, he had eleven children. According to the 1790 census, James Frisby is listed as the owner of thirty slaves, a large number for the times. Frisby left ownership of his estate to his three daughters when he died in 1807. The following year, two of Frisby's daughters sold their shares to the third, Rebecca Frisby Wilmer and her husband, the Reverend Simon Wilmer. Reverend Wilmer was an Episcopalian who studied for the ministry at the same Kent County church that his wife's illustrious grandfather, William, belonged to. He went on to serve as minister in several area parishes. Though he managed to offend an influential parishioner at one point with his progressive attitude toward the Episcopalian service, Wilmer was largely well-received as a minister.

Simon Wilmer sold Hinchingham in 1819 to John W. Wilmer of Baltimore City. Eventually, ownership of Hinchingham fell to the Gales, a well-known family in Kent County, in the mid-nineteenth century. The Gale family owned the estate for a quarter of a century. Today, Hinchingham belongs to famous modeling school and agency owner, Giorgio Piazzi, originally from Italy.

Hinchingham sits at the end of a long driveway on the west side of Maryland Route 445. The main block of the house, laid in Flemish bond, has two brick chimneys and a box cornice with identical moldings. There are 9/6 sash windows on the first floor, 6/6 sash windows on the second floor and in the three pedimented roof dormers. The one-and-a-half storey wing to the north has one brick chimney at the north end and a porch at both front and rear sides. There are two dormers. The date of construction, 1774, appears in large numerals executed in black headers on the southern end of the house.

The main block has a center hall plan with one room on each side. The south room has two circular headed cupboards with fluted pilasters, one on each side of the fireplace. The walls have panelled wainscoting below the chair rail and there is an ornamented ceiling cornice. The north room has a panelled chimney breast with a closet to the left. The stairway, guarded by a fine banister with a half-hand rail on the wall side, rises on the right to the upper floors. Much of the wing has been altered and modernized.

LAMB'S MEADOWS

Fairlee-Stillpond Road, Still Pond

Situated a mile and a half south of the Village of Still Pond, in a wide expanse of level fields, Lamb's Meadows reflects in its quiet architecture the character of its builder, Pearce Lamb, who was a member of the Society of Friends. Pearce Lamb received the original patent of Lamb's Range in 1683. This, it is believed, was added to Lamb's Meadows, which was granted to Pearce Lamb in 1694.

Pearce Lamb immigrated from Nottingham, England and arrived in Kent County in the mid 1600's. Owned by direct descendants of Pearce and Mary Lamb for nearly 300 years, Lamb's Meadows has survived with few architectural changes.

The dwelling is a small brick building with gambrel roof and a low kitchen wing. Prominent in the kitchen wing, in blue glazed brick, is the date 1733, indicating the year that this part of the house was built. It is believed that the main part of the dwelling was built in 1696. Three chimneys in Flemish bond rise from the brick walls and six typical Kent County flat roofed dormer windows admit light to the second floor bedrooms.

As is true of so many Quaker houses, there are two front doors, one entering the almost square living room and the other going into the dining room. There is a fireplace between two cupboards in the living room and the entire north wall is splendidly panelled to the ceiling. The solid doors of the cupboards are hung from the original hinges. There is no mantle over the arched brick fireplace, an earmark of early 17th and 18th century construction. In addition to the panelling there is a three foot wainscoting. Very beautiful random width floors remain on the first and second floors.

The dining room has no wainscoting but the ceiling and high panelling on the southern wall are almost identical with those in the living room. In place of the right hand cupboard there is a short passageway to a landing from which a flight of steps leads down to the kitchen. An extremely large fireplace with crane occupies the south wall of the kitchen. Prior to construction of the kitchen wing all meals were prepared in the large fireplace which still stands in the basement of the main section of the house.

Although more than a mile from the Sassafras River, Lamb's Meadows resembles the type of house usually found near the water. The flat dormer windows and the gambrel roof, the small size and the interior arrangement, are characteristic of shore architecture.

Lamb's Meadows is owned today by Mr. and Mrs. Omar R. Carrington, of Chevy Chase, Maryland. Mr. Carrington is a direct descendant of Pearce and Mary Lamb through his mother's family. Among their family possessions are sheets woven from flax grown at Lamb's Meadows. The farm contains 327 acres and has been managed by Mahlon and Betty Taylor for the last 30 years.

There are many old homes in Kent County, among which are the Comegys Bight House located on a recess in the Chester River (1768); Caulk's Field (1743); Knock's Folly, which has a beautifully panelled dining room; Hebron, built about 1713, near the source of Old Steelpoone Creek; and the Thomas Perkins House, erected in 1720. From a mill on this property flour was supplied to the army of General Washington at Valley Forge. The whole of storied Kent County is full of remarkable examples of early American architecture and an encyclopedia could be written on these houses alone.

WIDEHALL

101 Water Street, Chestertown

In Chestertown on the bank of the Chester River, is Widehall, one of the most beautiful homes on the Eastern Shore. It is of brick, two-and-a-half storeys in height, with a high basement. Its dormer windows and two storey porch command a fine view across the river.

Thomas Smyth bought the lot from the heirs of an estate. One of the heirs, William Granger, was only 20 and could not legally convey the title. So Smyth went to the Colonial Assembly to secure his title. The Act of the Assembly dated November 19, 1769 states "the said Thomas Smyth hath erected on said Lot a large and Valuable Brick House and kitchen which he was Desirous of finishing, etc." So the house was nearly finished before the title was cleared.

Thomas Smyth, having financial difficulties, sold it in 1790. In 1801 it was bought by Robert Wright, who became Senator and Governor of Maryland. He sold it in 1810 to Elizabeth Chambers. On July 24, 1822 it went to Ezekiel F. Chambers. He was a member of the U.S. Senate in the 1820s and later was a prominent Judge. At his death his executor sold it March 16, 1870 to Robert Clay Wright who only owned it one year but in that short time he did a great deal to spoil its Colonial Appearance.

November 27, 1871 George B. Westcott bought it. He owned it for many years, but apparently never lived there. He rented it to people—some of whom ran it as a boarding house so it became badly run down.

On March 20, 1909 Wilbur Watson Hubbard bought it from the Estate of Mr. Westcott. Mrs. Hubbard took great care to restore it. She was a pioneer in Colonial restoration. Now owned by their son Wilbur Ross Hubbard, who has completed further restorations and has it furnished with appropriate antiques, the mansion is once more among the great homes of the Eastern Shore of Maryland.

The front door is approached from the street by two flights of steps with a brick terrace between. The door which is of the best Georgian design opens on the wide hall from which the house received its name, that runs the depth of the building to the garden door opening on the river porch.

On the left is the stair hall, from which a wainscotted hanging staircase leads to the upper floors. Separating the halls are three arches which are unique in Colonial Maryland architecture. Another arch divides the main hall in half. On the right of the front door is the large drawing room lighted by tall windows. The fireplace, in the center of the partition between it and the living room, is also a restoration. The whole house is symmetrically arranged, in typical Georgian manner. In the dining room we find a slanted Wall-of-Troy moulding and panelling to the ceiling over the fireplace. This was not harmed during the many vicissitudes through which the house passed, and is as beautiful today as when it was first built by Thomas Smyth.

CLOVER FIELDS

Forman's Landing Road, Queenstown

Only a mile from Wye Mills, surrounded by shade trees and wide grounds, is the large Colonial residence known as Clover Fields. William Hemsley, who served as High Sheriff of Queen Anne's County in 1724, received the patent to the property six years later. Here the Hemsley family lived for many years as the tombstones in the private graveyard nearby testify. Some of the distinguished names on the stones are Lloyd, Tilghman, and Forman. The present owner of Clover Fields is the Thomas H. Callahan Estate.

The two-and-a-half storey mansion, which is supposed to have been built about 1730, of white painted brick, is very large and presents an appearance of even greater size. There are zigzag string courses and a glazed diamond pattern high in the wall facing Forman's Landing below. The chimneys of red brick are of the multiple type peculiar to the English Tudor style.

Architecturally speaking, Clover Fields offers various peculiarities of note. In the original plan two large first floor rooms were separated by a hall. At the end of the hall was a stair tower leading to the upper storeys. Behind the dwelling there was a separate brick kitchen, probably with a covered passage of some sort leading to the main building. All of this has since been connected and three new rooms added between the house and the kitchen.

On entering the front door from the broad front porch with its four white columns, a hall stretches to the stairs. On the right is the entrance to the large living room with its great projecting fireplaces. Facing the door to the living room is the door to the banquet hall, one of the finest in Maryland. Covered from floor to ceiling in large wood panels and with a beautifully balanced scheme of fenestration, this room presents an appearance which seems to demand festive garb. Over the large fireplace is a wood carving in relief of a hunting scene, the technique of which suggests that it was done by a native of Switzerland. A complicated moulding welds the panelling and ceiling together. Other decorative carving on the sides and above the mantel has been gilded and lends a touch of color to the white panels.

The stair tower is almost square, being eleven and a half by twelve and a half feet, and the steps wind about it interrupted by a landing at each corner. The entrance to the tower is guarded by jalousies with a sunburst pattern.

It is related that one of the inhabitants of Clover Fields had a great antipathy to being buried. He was so emphatic that he made the family promise that his body would lie above ground. Today, his tomb of red brick can be seen and in it, as he wished, lie his bones.

KENNERSLEY

Clabber Hill Road, Church Hill

With its pair of tall chimneys and center pediment Kennersley still looms over the junction of Island and Southeast creeks, near Church Hill, midway between Chestertown and Centreville. The house is withdrawn several hundred yards from the water and commands an extensive view of rolling country and the network of rivers which empty into a wide bay just off the Chester River.

Built circa 1785-1798 by Captain Richard Ireland Jones, is in the finest Maryland Colonial tradition, with a square central section flanked by wings connected to the main building by passageways. The entrance hall is wide and imposing, running the width of the main building. In the left hand corner there rises a beautifully designed stairway leading to the upper storeys. Well proportioned rooms with fourteen foot ceilings, graceful cornices, large fireplaces and lovely mantels, impart a dignity to the house which is further enhanced by careful restoration. It is the only surviving 18th Century five-part house in Queen Anne's County.

The date of the original grant to the property was previous to 1683; but the tax records do not show that there was a building there until 1704, indicating that some form of the dwelling was built the year before. Part of this structure may have been incorporated in the present house.

In 1785 or 1786 Richard Ireland Jones, Captain of a troop of horses attached to the Sixth Brigade of Queen Anne's County militia, married Susanna Carroll Tilghman, daughter of Colonel Edward Tilghman. At the time of their marriage, Susanna Carroll Tilghman owned a tract of 500 acres on South East Creek, near Church Hill. It was there that Jones built Kennersley. In 1798, the Federal Direct Tax listed Richard I. Jones as the owner of part of Tullies Delight, "on Island Creek neare the mouth." Included is the following description, which clearly shows that Kennersley was by then complete:

1 dwelling house 2 stories 35 × 35

2 brick covered passages leading to the wings,
1 of the wings 18 × 18 the other 35 × 18 brick

Richard and Susannah had one child, Arthur Tilghman Jones, born about the year 1787. Susannah died circa 1800 and left Kennersley to Arthur, but with a life interest to her husband, who later remarried.

James Bordley, Jr., in his detailed study of the Hollyday and related families, gives the following account of Arthur's ownership:

. . .Unfortunately, Arthur was a prodigal spender, and it was not long after his marriage that he was seriously involved financially. He mortgaged his home, the sheriff sold his wife's inherited slaves, he tried to buy his father's life interest so he could—and finally did sell "Kennersley." His father said of him, "His plans of today are but his dreams tomorrow." Visionary and not practical, his father said, "Only his use of whiskey keeps me from thinking him unbalanced." By 1820 he had exhausted his resources and was in debt to the extent of seventy thousand dollars. His father could not then assist him, because "Much of my fortune had been squandered in schemes invented by Arthur." Henry Hollyday, II, of "Ratcliffe," who was one of the principal creditors of both father and son, in the end had to take over "Kennersley" in 1827.

The will of Henry Hollyday was probated in 1850, and Kennersley descended to his heirs, Thomas R. Hollyday and others. In 1858 the property was conveyed to John H. Evans and in 1877 it was purchased by Dr. Washington Finley. Kennersley remained in the Finley family until 1913, when it was sold to William C. Hall. Hall in turn sold the property in 1933, and since that time the estate has passed through more than a dozen conveyances and the house has been extensively restored. In 1979, Kennersley was purchased by Mr. and Mrs. Warren J. Cox, the present owners.

MELFIELD

Corsica Neck Road, Centreville

Many of the well known homes in Queen Anne's County are situated along the Chesapeake Bay overlooking the water. However, when sites were found off the Chesapeake they were in rolling meadows and rich fields. One such home is Melfield, where the Earle family had been seated for many years. Other interesting places in the same county are Bowlingly, built 1733; Wheatlands, or Long Neglect; and Bloomingdale, which has an unusual hexagonal two storey porch over the entrance.

About two and a half miles from Centreville, on Corsica Neck between Tilghman Cove and Middle Quarter Cove on the Corsica River, stands the ancestral home of the Earle family. Built and owned by Judge James Tilghman of The Hermitage, it became an Earle property when Mary Tilghman, daughter of Judge James Tilghman, married Judge Richard Tilghman Earle. The place was given to his son, Samuel Thomas Earle, when he was a young man. He lived at Melfield for sixty-eight years before he died in 1904, survived by two daughters, Mrs. E.M. Forman and Mrs. P.H. Fedderman; and two sons, William Brundage Earle of Queen Anne's County, and Dr. Samuel T. Earle of Baltimore.

The property was divided into two farms; Dr. Earle receiving "Chatfield", the outer farm, his brother inheriting the home place. When William Brundage Earle died, his oldest son, William B. Earle, became the owner of Melfield. His brother, Swepson Earle, was the author of *The Chesapeake Bay Country* and *Maryland's Colonial Eastern Shore.* The current owner is J. Wallace Scott, Jr.

The house is one of the few in Maryland which has a porch two storeys high supported by great fluted columns. As a matter of fact, this was added some time before the War Between the States and is not indicative of the architectural leanings of the Colonial settlers. However, time has made the mansion into an integrated whole, the new blending smoothly with the old.

The front door opens directly into the dining room which has no panelling. The large fireplace and mantel are on the east wall, slightly off center, and in the far right corner is the door to the twenty foot square parlor. Here the fireplace is in the center of the west wall and another door gives on the front porch. Steps are tucked away in a wing and are strictly utilitarian. Behind this wing, which also has a fireplace, are the pantry and the big kitchen. Here there is another flight of stairs leading to the servants' quarters on the second floor.

A feature of this yellow two storey brick mansion is the chimney rising from the center of the main section, and the pediment and bull's-eye window on the west end of the house. Enormous columns and the presence of one of the largest oak trees in Maryland combine to dwarf the building proper.

There is a cemetery on the Melfield estate, surrounded by a chain link fence and flanked by corn fields. It is still well maintained by descendants of the Earle family. There are 43 headstones in this private burial ground, though Judge Richard Tilghman Earle himself is buried at Chesterfield Cemetery in Centreville.

OLD WYE

Queenstown

On a hill at the tip of the long neck which forms the southern boundary of Queen Anne's County, overlooking the water, stood Old Wye, which had been connected with the Paca family for many years. It was sometimes referred to as Paca Plantation. Although the house known as Old Wye no longer stands, there is a small private graveyard near the site where the body of Governor Paca rests under a rough-hewn granite memorial erected in 1911. The grave site has been surrounded with a sturdy, yet ornate fence.

The tract originally was granted to William Coursey, after whose death it passed through several hands before it came into the possession of Colonel Edward Tilghman. He built Old Wye some time between 1740 and 1745. Colonel Tilghman, distinguished for his precocious and versatile mind, was appointed High Sheriff of Queen Anne's County at the early age of twenty-six.

There is no proof of the manner in which the property became a Paca holding, but the most generally accepted theory is that Juliana Tilghman married John Paca and brought the grant as her dowry. It remained in the Paca family for many years, but in 1877 was listed as being owned by Dr. W.H. DeCoursey. This was shortly after a double murder at Old Wye which rocked county society to its foundation. What seemed to be a sequel was the burning across the river of the great Italian villa, Wye Hall, owned by another branch of the Paca family and sometimes confused with Old Wye.

Other owners of the property have been Edwin D. Morgan of Long Island, who purchased it in 1931, and Robert F. Gibson of Centreville, Maryland. In 1937, the house and property were purchased by Mr. and Mrs. Arthur Houghton, then of New York City.

The design of the house was of that individualistic type which springs directly from the soil. Although built in the time when the influence of the Georgian period was strongly felt in the Province, the exterior of Old Wye reflected the Maryland planters' tastes rather than those of the builders of great country mansions which were being erected elsewhere.

The first impression was that of a long low dwelling, at one end of which there was a building with two chimneys rising from the flattened ends of the roof and dormer windows which did not break the line of the gambrel roof. The long addition on the left was made up of kitchens, storehouses, servants' quarters, and a room containing a great Dutch oven. All the floors here were of carefully laid bricks. In order that the steaming dishes from the cook's hands did not go into the open air before being served at the table, the entire front of the addition was covered by an elongation of the shingled roof line coming down so low that it nearly touched the ground.

The interior was divided unequally by a large hall in which rose the fine stairway to the second storey. In the rooms on that first floor were corner fireplaces. Panelling was found over the fireplace in the large square parlor on the right, and in the same position in the dining room on the other side of the hall.

Mr. Houghton also purchased additional surrounding properties and consolidated them into what is now known as Wye Plantation. The Houghtons never actually lived in Old Wye, though they did use part of the home for guests. He had an architectural survey completed by the firm which designed Colonial Williamsburg, and Old Wye was deemed as not suitable for his needs. He did have a library with living accommodations built on the property, while he maintained his New York residence. When he began planning his retirement, around 1970, Old Wye was torn down, and the current manor house was completed in 1972. The Houghtons turned the house over to the Aspen Institute in 1982, for use as a conference center. They have restored the guest house which had been the overseer's cottage, built in 1690.

WALNUT GROVE

Wright's Neck Road, Centreville

On Reeds Creek across from Tilghman Neck and six miles from Centreville, there is a small dwelling called Walnut Grove. The trees from which its name was taken have disappeared, but the sturdy little house still lifts its beautifully fitted brick ends of sparkling Flemish bond to the skies.

One of the oldest houses in Queen Anne's County, it was built in 1684. The tract originally was taken up by Thomas Hynson, but his son-in-law, Solomon Wright, had it resurveyed in 1685 and called it Warplesdon. It had been in the Wright family for many years. After Dorsey Wright owned Walnut Grove in the 1930's, it was acquired by the Meyers' family, who in turn sold it to Gloria Churchill. She sold it to a group of Philadelphia investors, who used Walnut Grove as a weekend retreat and hunting lodge. Their sons began restoration of the home in 1983. The tillable portion of the 280 acre property has been farmed through the succession of owners by David Clark since 1957.

The building is only one-and-a-half storeys high with dormer windows. The front and rear walls are of hand-hewn squared poplar logs with plaster between, the former being covered with clapboard, the latter with hand-riven shingles over which clapboard has been placed. Porches are both back and front, and the roof is shingled. There are only three very small windows of four panes each on the west end, and two windows each for the front and back. A modern dining room and kitchen have been added to the eastern end.

The front door gives directly into the large living room. At one time this was beautifully panelled to the ceiling, but all the woodwork was sold to be installed in a Long Island country house. No panelling remains on the ground floor, but some original rough wainscoting on the second floor is still in place. On the left of the living room is the fireplace with its square deep opening flanked on its right by an inset rounded cupboard, and on the other side by a square cupboard lighted by a small window.

The steps to the second floor are on the right, separated from the living room by a partition. Here is an example of an early enclosed stairway, which does not cross over the fireplace in the chimney arrangement. There is some reason to believe that the steps were added after the second storey was made habitable.

In line with the front door appears the entrance to the long narrow kitchen. This has a great corner fireplace with a small cupboard above it. As in practically all of the early manor houses, doors and windows are placed to allow what breezes there were in summer to flow freely through the house.

Near Walnut Grove is Reed's Creek, built by Colonel Thomas Wright about 1775. The large two storey mansion when contrasted to Walnut Grove is a fine example of the changes that a century of building can make in homes in the same neighborhood. Reed's Creek evidently was laid out according to a definite plan, while Walnut Grove seems to have sprouted spontaneously from the rich soil of Queen Anne's County.

OAK LAWN

Route 312, Ridgely

Caroline County is provided with an outlet to the Chesapeake Bay by the winding Choptank River. Most of the great mansions of this county are scattered along its banks; however, there are exceptions, one of which is Oak Lawn. Near the present town of Denton and two and a half miles from Ridgely, Benjamin Sylvester built this Colonial home, far from the water and in the midst of wide fields, in 1783. To leave his mark on the house, this gentleman placed in the north gable of the house the legend "B.S. 1783", carved in a round slab of wood. When this was blown down, the present tenant had it replaced in concrete with a facsimile of the original writing.

The builder left the property to his granddaughter, Mrs. Mary M. Bourne, in 1797, with Isaac Purnell as executor. Mrs. Bourne died in 1881, and in later years the mansion passed through many hands. For some time Senator John F. Dawson owned the land, so that it is sometimes spoken of as Dawson's Farm. Others who have had the property in their possession have been T.W. Jones, J.K. Lynch, and Ambrose Lucas. The present owner is Mrs. Edith D. Connolly of Queen Anne.

The front has a large porch reached by steps, the bottom one of which is a mill stone. The front facade is divided in the usual Georgian style, a door in the center with two windows on either side. A central hall bisects the main section of Oak Lawn. On the right side is the entrance to the library, where there is a three foot wainscoting running around the walls. In the far corner is a fireplace. Opposite the door to the library is the entrance to the sitting room or parlor which has a corner fireplace and a three foot wainscoting.

Half-way down the hall is an arch beyond which, on the right, are the stairs to the upper floors. The balustrade of the steps is like that of Bohemia, Chinese Chippendale in design. The door to the present kitchen is at the foot of the stairs. Opposite is the entrance to the dining room with a corner fireplace.

The most interesting feature of Oak Lawn is the brick colonnade opening from the kitchen and leading to the two storey brick servants' quarters. This is one of the few original arcades still standing in Maryland. There are stories which would lead to the belief that almost all of the houses built in the last three decades of the eighteenth century had a similar passage, but so few are left that they are thought to be only a hall between a wing and the main building. However, it is probable that actual colonnades did exist, but have disappeared in the present day, when the tendency is toward a unified unit home rather than a central mansion surrounded by many outbuildings.

There is a legend that chains have been heard to clank on the stairs of Oak Lawn and it is true that there was an authentic dungeon deep in the cellar, but today the chains are never heard and the dungeon, alas, is the abode of a pipeless hot air heater, which is no longer used. The present occupants use woodstoves to heat several rooms of Oak Lawn.

POTTER HALL

Martin Lane, Denton

In Caroline County on the Eastern Shore of Maryland, a mile and a half below Watt's Creek on the Choptank River, stands the two-and-a-half storey brick mansion known as Potter Hall. This telescopic house of three diminishing sections lies on a fifty foot bluff in a horseshoe bend of the river, commanding an extensive view up and down a stream which is deep enough to allow ocean going vessels to dock at Potter's Landing below.

Some time before 1730 Zabdiel Potter, a sea captain from Rhode Island, sailed up the Choptank and was instantly captivated by the charm of the scenery. He settled near "Coquericus Fields," so called from the stream of that name, which has since disappeared. The captain commanded one of the vessels which carried cargo from the enterprising village of Potter's Landing directly to British ports. On one of these voyages, in 1760, the gallant sailer met his death. He was survived by two sons, Dr. Zabdiel Potter and Nathaniel Potter.

Nathaniel died without issue in 1783, ten years before his brother. Zabdiel had two sons, Nathaniel and William. The first was a founder of the University of Maryland Medical School and a well known doctor and teacher. His brother, General William Potter, built the larger part of Potter Hall in 1808, and died there in 1847. Both he and his wife were buried near the house but their graves were moved to the Denton Cemetery some forty or fifty years ago. William Potter gained many honors, serving as Brigadier-General in the Maryland Militia, thrice on the Governor's Council, and many times as a member of the legislature. His one son, Zabdiel Webb Potter, died in 1855.

Potter Hall was evidently meant to be approached from the river, as the front door and the steps to the upper storeys are on this side. Huge fireplaces are in each room, and in the smaller and older wing, the walls are very thick and the ceilings low. No chair rails or fanlighted doors such as adorn the large wing can be found here. All is New England simplicity; there are only two rooms and a steep dark stairway to the second-floor. Dormer windows light the attic.

The nineteenth century wing is larger and more pretentious. The mahogany banistered stairs rise on the right, and plain mouldings and conservative spindles set the style. The only place in which the architect allowed his imagination any play was in the step-ends which have cautious scrolls, beautifully executed. None of the rooms is panelled.

A large mantel is in the room on the left of the hall, and in the library immediately behind is a fine mantel flanked by panelled cupboards built into the wall. The second floor is practically identical with the first, and the large attic is lighted by four dormer windows.

At one time Potter Hall was the country home of Colonel Frederick F. Lyden of New York who was born at Potter's Landing in 1869. The next owner was Hugh S. Fullerton who sold the property to the present owners Dr. and Mrs. Monroe H. Martin in 1953. They retired to Potter Hall in 1971 from College Park where Dr. Martin was Professor of Mathematics at the University of Maryland, the same institution in which Dr. Nathaniel Potter, mentioned above, played such an important role, an interesting coincidence.

HAMPDEN

Island Creek Road South, Trappe

Thomas Martin, born in 1629 at Park Place, Dorsetshire, England, came to Maryland in 1663 and in that year built Hampden, the first brick house in Talbot County, on two hundred acres of land purchased from Edward Lloyd. For over two hundred years Martins lived at Hampden, taking an important place in the life of the county and serving their country with distinction.

Hampden is on Dividing Creek between Sawmill Cove and Leonard Cove, in a small grove. It is not a large house, being but one-and-a-half storeys of brick, with dormer windows. Today the property is owned by Thomas Firth, who makes his home there.

The house is built in two sections of unequal size, with two brick chimneys on the larger and one on the smaller, or kitchen, end. The front door, which once had a porch, opens on a dark hall running through the house to the back door, panelled on the outside and diagonally battened on the inside. Half-way down the hall the staircase rises on the right; the walls are wainscoted to three feet, above which is plaster to the plaster ceiling. The banister rail is exceptionally wide, broadening at the bottom to cover the cluster of four balustrades at the foot of the steps. The under side of the stairs has large panels and the step-ends are decorated with ogee arches.

On the left hand side of the hall half-way down is the door to the living room, sixteen and a half feet by nineteen and a half feet (the depth of the house). An enormous fireplace takes up the greater part of the south wall. Once there were cupboards on either side which have been torn out. The walls are panelled to the ceiling, and the windows are splayed in with deep window seats that project into the room.

On the right of the hall is the door to the square dining room which has a fireplace across the far corner. The windows, splayed in, and the window seats, are of the same pattern as those in the living room. On the left is the door to the first floor bedroom, which also has a corner fireplace back to back with the one in the dining room. Between this room and the hall is a very short low passageway under the stair landing. A door from the dining room opens on the kitchen, where a large fireplace has been abandoned in favor of a modern stove.

Hampden has been completely restored and been included on the Maryland House and Garden Pilgrimage itinerary many times during the past twenty years. A wing has been added off the kitchen end, which is attached by a breezeway. It is modelled after a Williamsburg outbuilding.

LONG POINT

Route 579, Neavitt

Facing Balls Creek where Broad Creek runs into it, almost at the end of Nelson Point and one mile southeast of the Neavitt Post Office, stands Long Point. The original grant was made to Ralph Elston in 1663, and it is believed that he built the existing brick dwelling about 1681 over the foundations of an earlier structure. There is no doubt about its antiquity or about the thickness of the walls, which were cut through to make a door at one end. Three and a half feet of brick at a point above the foundations show that Mr. Elston intended his home to stand for a long time.

Over the years more rooms were added to the land side, completely changing that end. The original structure is two storeys high with an attic and gambrel roof with dormer windows. The handmade whitewashed bricks are much larger than is usual. There is evidence that there was at one time an extensive boxwood garden around what was a family burial ground.

The fenestration is balanced, with a door flanked by a window on either side, and the same arrangement is used on the other side of the building. The interior is one huge room, originally with great fireplaces at either end, but only one remains because the other has been turned into the newer part of the house. The graceful mantle of the remaining fireplace is hand carved, carefully apportioned to space. On the right is the winding and closed stairway, twisting over the fireplace to the rooms above; a cupboard balances it on the other side, the whole end of the room being panelled to the ceiling. The opposite end of the room is similarly panelled with a cupboard to the right and on the left, the door which was cut through to the modern part of the house. There is a commodious cellar running under the whole building, a rather novel feature in such an early house. It is entered by a large square door on the water end of the dwelling.

Ralph Eston married Mary, widow of John Ball in 1694. They had no children and Benjamin Ball inherited. Some time before 1720 he conveyed Long Point, as well as other properties, to his brother, Lieutenant Thomas Ball, and went to Kent Island where he died some eight years later. In 1772, Lieutenant Ball died, and his children, John and Mary, came into possession. William Shield, of Kent County, bought Long Point and lived there with his wife, a great-granddaughter of the first Mary Ball, until 1800, when a member of the Harrison family acquired the property. This family lived in the house for over a hundred years. It was then used as a hunting club for a number of years and subsequently changed ownership several times.

Long Point was acquired in 1966 by Carol and Rex Kilbourn, Jr. and became the home of his parents, Alverta and Rex Kilbourn, Sr. Ralph Eston built lastingly, and the Kilbourn seniors have worked lovingly to maintain Long Point as one of Talbot County's modest showplaces.

MYRTLE GROVE

Goldsborough Neck Road, Easton

Six miles from Easton, at the junction of the Miles River and Goldsborough Creek is Myrtle Grove. The original frame, one-and-a-half storey building was put up in 1734 by Robert Goldsborough, son of Robert of Ashby, and the larger brick wing added in 1790.

Robert Goldsborough's son, Judge Robert Goldsborough, inherited the property, willing it to his son, Senator Robert Henry Goldsborough, who was the father of six children. The house was owned by each in turn, the last being George, who left it to the children of his brother William. Charles Goldsborough, the last of these, died without a will; and the children of his sister, Mrs. Daniel Henry, inherited the land. The property is now in the possession of Margaret H. Donoho, daughter of Robert Goldsborough Henry, and her husband John.

The entrance road is lined with gnarled cedars, terminating in a circular driveway which sweeps before the steps leading up to the front door. The door opens under the stairway into a wide hall with a plaster cornice and a chair rail. The steps, edged with a simple balustrade, rise unsupported on the right, the riser of each made of a single piece of fitted wood built into the wall. At the end of the hall is the river door opening toward the water. On the immediate left is the door to the parlor which has a large mantel flanked by a single cupboard on the right. A chair rail and an ornate plaster moulding, and hangings in red damask and gold, bring back the past so vividly that a motor-car, glimpsed through the windows, seems out of place. In the sitting room, which can be entered either from the hall or from the parlor, the hangings are the same and the moulding is a little more elaborate, as is the mantel. There is also a chair rail.

At the foot of the stairs is a door to the porch of the older building. Wooden pillars rise from the brick floor, flush with the ground, and support the roof of the porch. Immediately inside, narrow enclosed steps lead to the upper floors. On the left is a wall panelled to the ceiling, at the end of which is the door to the library, one of the loveliest rooms in Maryland. Panelled to the ceiling on two sides and tinted green, this is the heart of a living home. The fireplace has no mantel. The panelling is in squares, rectangles, and balanced designs in curves on rectangles. Across the hall is the dining room. Here there is a fireplace with no mantel, panelled to the ceiling, and cream tinted walls which reflect soft light upon the portraits of the Goldsborough family. From this room doors lead to the modern kitchen wing.

At the southern end of the exterior is a projecting pediment cornice decorated with consoles and dentils. Myrtle Grove has a setting worthy of its architectural excellence. Gardens and trees are so tastefully arranged that they achieve a natural unity with the mansion. The water on three sides adds a final touch to the already arresting beauty of Myrtle Grove.

OTWELL

Otwell Road, Oxford

Otwell, one of the few earliest properties recorded in Talbot County, stands on a peninsula between Easton and Oxford. It is bounded on the east and south by Goldsborough Creek, on the west by Tred Avon River and on the north by Trippe Creek. For over three hundred years it has been a farm and has been owned by only six families. It will always be known as "home of the Goldsboroughs", who owned it from 1722 to 1946.

On August 15, 1659, the original tract of 500 acres was surveyed for William Taylor, who constructed a one room frame house, with large fireplace, a few yards north of the present "T" wing, and lived there while work was done on a more fitting brick home. Eleanor Goldsborough Bartlett Therien records the date of 1662 for the brick house.

Taylor's house was a storey and a half, set on a foundation of native field stone, (still visible in the basement), two large flush chimneys and a steeply pointed roof covered with 3' long split oak shingles, feathered and secured with hand made nails. Bricks were of native clay, fired on the place. The house faced west toward the Tred Avon River and consisted of "an office and a greate room", each with its own fireplace.

At his death in 1687, William Taylor left Otwell to his son, Samuel, who sold it that year to Colonel Vincent Lowe. Three years later Lowe bequeathed it to Foster Turbutt, oldest son of his wife's sister, Sarah Foster Turbutt. Young Turbutt became Clerk of the Court, lived at Otwell 30 years and raised a family that became prominent in the county. When he died in 1720 the property passed to his son, Henry, 12 years of age, who died 2 years later, making his sister, Sarah, 14, the new owner. Sarah had married Nicholas Goldsborough III, of Peck's Point in 1721. When she and Nicholas set up housekeeping at Otwell in 1722, they established the Goldsborough connection that lasted for 224 years and produced a line of eminent individuals who distinguished themselves in both private and public life.

During the years 1722-25, Nicholas and Sarah changed the axis of the house to north-south and started the tail of the "T" by adding a spacious hall with a door at each end, one step lower than the original house floor, and a large room beyond with a very large fireplace. Black walnut cut on the place was used for beams, window frames, doors and the graceful stairway with a tulip carved on the end of each step.

When Matthew Tilghman Goldsborough died in 1928, his daughter, Margaret Ward Goldsborough became the new owner and continued to live there for 18 years. In 1946 she sold to Mr. and Mrs. Andrew Porter of Philadelphia. They renovated the interior, lowered the dirt floor of the basement to accommodate furnace, pipes etc., for central heating and modern plumbing. They razed many of the old buildings, built the small log house, the service court, garage, barns and large swimming pool.

In 1957 the Porters sold to Mr. and Mrs. John E. Jackson of Pittsburgh. Soon after renovation was begun a disastrous fire destroyed the original wing, the hall and the bedroom over the dining room. With careful research, and the help of Ian Crawford MacCallum, a knowledgeable architect, the walls were rebuilt of the old brick, other details restored and the famous tulip stairway faithfully reproduced in black walnut. Two fireplaces were eliminated, a new entrance designed for the land side, and an enclosed porch added to the water side. The kitchen was completely remodeled and central air conditioning installed. Roads were paved, and new farm buildings constructed for a working farm and commercial dairy. Two small buildings were made into attractive residences, and space over the 4 car garage was converted into a lodge.

When Mr. Jackson died in 1971, his widow continued to live there. She has done a number of things to preserve and protect the property. There are deed restrictions against sub-divisions near the main house. The water and land surrounding it are a wildlife refuge and the 100 acre tract of woods along the main driveway has been deeded to the Nature Conservancy.

PRESQU'ILE-ON-WYE

Presqu'ile Road, Easton

The meandering Wye River, on its way to the broad waters of the Chesapeake Bay, affords many beautiful building sites. One of the most notable of these is occupied by Presqu'ile, a show-place of the Eastern Shore. The charming name evidently was chosen because the property is almost surrounded by water.

Smooth green lawns reach down to the softly lapping waters of the river and many splendid trees provide ample shade. A recent tasteful planting of shrubs and flowers has replaced the formal English gardens of yester-year. This background makes an ideal setting for the lovely, spacious white house with its cool screened porches and jutting wings.

The dwelling is built of clapboard; and the double-entrance doors, both front and back, are interestingly panelled in natural wood. The central hall, which is panelled to the chair rail, runs all the way through the house. The stairway, with its fine hand-carved mahogany rail, rises two storeys from a well opening off the middle of the hall. The interior as a whole has been modernized for gracious living without losing its old-time charm and character.

The land, patented by Richard Woolman August 8th, 1662, was originally known as "Woolman's Land"; it was later sold into the Lloyd family, and became part of the great acreage owned by this distinguished Maryland family. The first Lloyds were puritans and merchants who came to Maryland from around Norfolk, Virginia. The well-known Wye House was their home and main estate. The house at Presqu'ile was built by Murray Lloyd, son of Governor Lloyd, in 1832.

This gentleman had two sons, one of whom was killed at Gettysburg; the other died of typhoid. Murray Lloyd sold Presqu'ile to his brother Edward Lloyd VI; from him it went to Colonel Lloyd VII (1825-1907), son of Edward Lloyd VI. Colonel Lloyd VII was born in Baltimore at the home of his grandparents. Private tutors gave him his early education. He later entered Princeton, but preferred a life of activity, and did not complete the course. He decided to follow the calling of his forefathers, that of the farmer, and soon after leaving college he took charge of one or more of his father's farms, living at Presqu'ile.

In 1877 he was chosen president of the state senate, and also had the largest farm in Talbot County. After the death of Colonel Lloyd VI, Colonel Lloyd VII went to live at Wye House, and Presqu'ile was inherited by his sister, Mrs. Key, who was Elizabeth Lloyd, and who married at Presqu'ile to the son of Francis Scott Key. The property was next deeded to Alicia Winder in 1887, and confirmed by Edward Lloyd Key, Mary T. Key, Alicia McB. Key, Francis S. Key, and Beatrice T. Key, in 1892. After Presqu'ile had changed owners several more times, Mr. and Mrs. Nils Anderson, of New York, took title in 1938.

Presqu'ile was purchased in 1953 by Mr. & Mrs. Rogers Clark Ballard Morton, who moved there from Louisville, Kentucky. After farming on the Eastern Shore for eight years, Mr. Morton was elected to Congress as the Representative of Maryland's first district. He served in this capacity for four terms and was re-elected to a fifth term. At this time, he was appointed Secretary of the Interior, a post he held for four years, following which he served as Secretary of Commerce for one year. He died in 1979. Mrs. Morton was remarried in 1981 to John Robbins Kimberly of Carmichael Farm in Queen Anne's County. Presqu'ile is presently occupied by Mr. & Mrs. Kimberly.

RATCLIFFE MANOR

off Route 33, Easton

In 1749 Henry Hollyday decided to take unto himself a bride, one Anna Maria Robins, and in order that she might have a suitable home he built Ratcliffe Manor. This brick mansion, on the north side of the Tred Avon River above Peach Blossom Creek, is one of the finest on the Eastern Shore and has a garden of English boxwood of astonishing height and extent. Ancient trees cast intricate shadows over the Flemish bond and add depth to a picture conceived in the middle of the eighteenth century and as charming today as it was then.

The proportions of the house are very fine; two chimneys on the right are balanced by two on the left and the roof is flattened at either end of the ridge, adding to the quaintness of the roof line. The entrance is a small pedimented portico with two columns and two benches. The white panelled door opens into a square hall, on the right of which the stairs rise to the upper floors of the house. The step-ends are decorated with a single and effective wave pattern. On the left is the door to the library. The door to the garden, directly in line with the front door, affords an admirable vista through the house, and like all the doors in the house, retains its original lock. A fireplace is across the far corner and the walls are wainscoted to three feet.

The living room, which may be gained from the library or from the hall, is one of the finest examples of eighteenth century panelling in Maryland. From floor to ceiling the walls are covered with wide panels, which break into two alcoves on the fireplace end, one with a window in it, and the other now converted into an open bookcase. Over the fireplace hangs an old portrait, giving the final touch to a room which must have been the pride and joy of Anna Maria. A treasure of this room is the mirror which hangs on the wall in the position for which it was designed by the firm of Thomas Chippendale in London.

The square dining room has a large projecting fireplace and a chair rail running around all four walls. A door to the servants' quarters, pantries and kitchen, opens from this room. There are two minor staircases in the house, perhaps to insure that the servants did not intrude on the gentry.

Henry Hollyday originally planned to leave Ratcliffe to his oldest son, Thomas, but his "conduct and deportment" was so deplorable that the will was changed and the property was left to another son, Henry. He died in 1850, and Richard C. Hollyday became the owner. His widow, Marietta, married Senator Charles Hopper Gibson and sold the house to A.A. Hathaway. Fire ravaged the kitchen, later restored in 1935, prior to the subsequent sale to John McCoy, executive director of the Du Pont Corporation. The present owner, Ambassador Gerard C. Smith, acquired Ratcliffe Manor in 1945.

WYE HOUSE

Bruff's Island Road, Easton

Where Shaw Bay and Lloyd Creek empty into the Wye River there is a broad point of land upon which is situated the seat of the Lloyd family, Wye House. The first Lloyd came to America and settled in Virginia in 1623 but removed to Maryland in 1649, taking up his residence in what was to be Anne Arundel County. When Talbot County was reorganized in 1662, Edward Lloyd settled there, as he had large estates in that county. The mansion he built, which he called Wye House, was destroyed by fire, some believing that the British burned it in 1781, others contending the date was 1814. The present house, now owned by Mrs. Elizabeth Lloyd Schiller, the ninth generation of Lloyds to live at Wye House, was erected somewhat previous to 1792, as there is a window pane with that date and the names Edward Lloyd and Eliza Lloyd scratched on it. Therefore, the 1814 date does not seem authentic.

Wye House is approached by an avenue of large trees leading to a circular driveway which sweeps up to the small columned entrance porch. The house is composed of a central section with balancing wings connected by smaller wings. Four great chimneys rise from the two-and-a-half storey main building, while the end wings have two chimneys. The fanlighted front door opens on a large hall with a small office on the right. On the left is the entrance to the south parlor where the mantel wall is panelled to the ceiling. Half way down the hall on the right is the opening to the stairwell.

The house is divided by two axes, one running the width of the building through the front door to the huge north parlor, the door of which is directly in line with the center garden window. The other axis is a hall which runs the length of the mansion, ending in the library on the left and the pantry on the right. Under the steps is the entrance to the servants' quarters and the kitchen. The door to the large cellar is in this section of the house.

The dining room opens on the hall and also, by a curious flattened arched door, into the north parlor which is large enough to be called a ballroom. Both rooms have fireplaces and a porch runs outside. In the west wing are living quarters and the library.

There is no more illustrious family in the history of Maryland than the Lloyds. Reputedly among the richest of the colonists, it is not strange that the extent of their holdings is unknown, but such titles as "Edward the Magnificent" would lend credence to the belief that they lived and acted like kings. However, the Lloyds were patriots and threw their considerable influence on the side of the Revolution.

One of the most noted buildings on the Wye property is the orangery, the only original one of its period still standing in Maryland. This beautifully proportioned cut-stone edifice looks as though it came directly from France. There is every reason to believe it is much older than the present house, as it is out of line with the main building which is in itself almost fanatically balanced. Another structure, of wood, on the right of Wye House, has been called an early blockhouse because of its curious construction, but, alas for romance, it is merely a smoke house.

CARTHAGENA

Myrtle Avenue, Secretary

Carthagena was one of the most luxurious homes of its day. Located at the fork of Secretary Creek, this property was known incorrectly for a time as "My Lady Sewall Manor." Dorchester County historian Elias Jones created this myth in 1925, perpetuating confusion about the original owners of this tract of land.

Actually, Carthagena's history began in 1675 when Thomas Taylor acquired 1,010 acres in the fork of Secretary Creek and called the parcel "Bath." He later acquired 622 acres that he called "Addition to Bath." Taylor deeded both tracts to son, Peter, who in turn deeded some acreage to his brother, Philip, and John Rye. Part of "Bath" was later taken in to the Choptank Indian Reservation. In 1726, John Anderton acquired 151 acres of that land from the Indians. The following year, Henry Trippe II acquired 500 additional acres of "Bath" from the Indians. In 1720, Trippe bought the parcel John Rye had owned from Rye's sister. Trippe then left ownership of his portion of "Bath" and "Addition to Bath" to his son, Henry Trippe III in 1723. Henry Trippe III proceeded to add to the land he had inherited. In 1740, he had the property resurveyed into a 1,250 acre tract which he called "Carthagena."

According to the 1763 will of Henry Trippe III, he was living at Carthagena at that time. John Andertons' descendents also owned a part of the "Bath" tract then. The exact date of the Carthagena building's construction is unknown, but it is likely that Henry Trippe had the house erected sometime in the early to mid-eighteenth century. Trippe was an important political figure at that time.

Carthagena belonged to descendents of Henry Trippe through the early part of the nineteenth century. The Carthagena tract was subsequently divided up and held among many different owners during the nineteenth and early part of the twentieth centuries. Today, Carthagena belongs to the Roman Catholic Church and is used as the Rectory of Our Lady of Good Counsel and the residence of the Reverend Edward J. Kaczorowski, Pastor. The original building has been restored and two modern wings have been added.

Carthagena is a one-and-a-half storey brick house. The main portion of the house is laid in Flemish bond. There is a central entrance, flanked by a single window on each side. There are three dormers on the "A" roof; a large brick chimney rises on the north gable.

The first floor is a single room, with a stairway ascending in the south west corner. Originally, the floor plan consisted of a large room which extended about two thirds the length of the house, with the stair hall located in the south west corner and a smaller room with a corner fireplace opening into the stair hall. The original mouldings have not been reproduced.

The second storey consists of a large bedroom and bath. Formerly, it was divided into three bedrooms and a corridor. The walls were composed of vertical, feather-edge panelling without moulding. A fielded panel was located above the four-panel door. These walls have been incorporated into the closet walls and bath wall. The hinges have foliated ends commonly found in the early eighteenth century.

One of the most notable features of early Carthagena was its extraordinary panelling. Though it is no longer a part of the house, the panelling belonging in Carthagena is on display at the Brooklyn Museum of Art. Mary A. Conkle, who owned the house in the early twentieth century, sold the wood to the museum in 1917.

Historians believe Carthagena is comparable in age to Castle Haven, also in Dorchester County.

CASTLE HAVEN

Castle Haven Road, Cambridge

Castle Haven is one of the best known landmarks in Dorchester County. The home is situated at the top of Castle Haven Point on the Choptank River, overlooking LeCompte Bay. The building dates back to the second quarter of the eighteenth century.

A tract of land called Antonine was originally patented to Frenchman Anthony LeCompte in 1659. Sometime around 1730, the house called Castle Haven was built on a parcel of Antonine, though the builder is unknown. Ownership of the land and the home from LeCompte's time until recently is not entirely clear. "Castle Haven" appears in the will of John Whitley in 1701. Around 1818, the Reverend James Kemp, Bishop of Maryland sold the land and the home to Levin and Mary Jones. Later, Thomas King Carroll used Castle Haven as his summer home, most likely around the mid-nineteenth century. After Carroll, Wilbur F. Jackson owned the house and enlarged it. The home subsequently had several more owners, the latest of which have been Dr. Raymond D. Menton, Jr., and Mr. James Mosteler.

The house is a large brick structure with three brick wings and a frame wing. The central part of the house is the earliest section of the building. Originally, this section was five bays long, two storeys high, though alterations and additions have changed its appearance somewhat. Off the north wing, there now stands a one story hyphen that houses the kitchen.

The walls of the main part of the house are laid in Flemish bond above the water table and English bond below. Cornices added in the nineteenth century hide segmental arches above the window. The east door frame is original; yet the window frames are of a later period. All windows have 1/1 sash and louvered shutters. The roof is a moderately-pitched "A," upon which chimneys stand at each end.

Each wing is built close to the ground so that the two full storeys are lower than the main cornice. The wings have a frieze and dentils of brick. One of the more recent owners has added a picture window in the north wing to afford a view of the river from the dining room. The entrance wing is square and lower than the others. There is a circular window above the door and a porch in front of the door.

Inside, the house is divided into a den and parlor separated by a passage in the earliest block and a stair hall in the west entrance wing, a billiard room in the south wing and the dining room in the north wing.

The parlor retains some handsome panelling from the second quarter of the eighteenth century, though only the panelling above the fireplace is in its original location. Panelled window seats also appear to be original. The panelling above the fireplace consists of a large raised panel flanked by short, stubby pilasters and three raised panels below. The sides of the fireplace are also panelled. Bold bolection moulding appears around the fireplace opening. Door and window trim is smaller scale bolection.

On the north side of the corridor is the den. Most likely, from indications in the cellar, this was originally two rooms with corner fireplaces. Both billiard room and dining room are plain inside, with back-to-back fireplaces.

There are several bedrooms, baths, and a porch located upstairs, though none has its original woodwork. A large attic extends across the house and is lighted by two windows on each gable. Two doors in the attic are original, from the earliest part of the building.

FRIENDSHIP HALL

Route 14, East New Market

On the outskirts of the small town of East New Market is Friendship Hall. This beautifully designed brick mansion is an excellent example of a Maryland Colonial home. It is composed of a large two storey building and a sizable wing at right angles, connected to the main section by a one storey wing.

Friendship Hall was erected by a Sullivane of Ireland about 1745. Buckland, across the way from Friendship Hall, was built by members of the same family, and the buildings have common architectural characteristics.

The house is approached from the main road by a straight driveway and stands in a flat meadow where shade trees are set about in seeming carelessness. Ivy mantles the mellow brick and breaks the facade into a pleasing pattern of green leaves and deep shadow. The interesting bold brick pilasters supporting the string course act as a border which frames the house like a picture.

The front door opens into a hall with a three foot wainscoting. On the left, the broad stairs rise; in line with the front door is an archway framing the garden doorway at the end of the hall. On the right of the hall is the door to the large square Great Hall with its panelled corner fireplace and wainscoting. This room opens into a small library, also with a corner fireplace. Across the hall lies a first floor formal dining room, which has a curious mantel arrangement; the panelling is so placed as to allow two doors to open into little cupboards.

From a small hall next to the long narrow pantry, three steps lead down to the large cheery summer dining room, off which the old kitchen opens. Here, jutting out into the room, is an enormous fireplace which suggests the bastion of an old Assyrian fortress.

There are many fine old homesteads in Dorchester County. John's Point, now destroyed, was built around 1666 on Tobacco Stick Creek. Judging from the restoration by Henry Chandlee Forman, as shown in "Early Manor and Plantation Houses of Maryland", this was a most interesting building, with windows wider than high, a roof line like that of Old Wye in Queen Anne's County, and two front doors. Spocot, built about 1662, by Stephen Gary, is one-and-a-half storeys high with dormer windows, and is entirely different from John's Point. The arrangement of the rooms, too, differs from Friendship Hall. The hundred years separating its building from the other two houses show the enormous strides taken by the people who were regarded as settlers. From immigrant settlements to new nation in little more than a century is indeed a long step. Curiously enough, houses have not progressed greatly since then, and Friendship Hall is the type of dwelling after which a great many of our smartest new suburban homes have been modeled.

Friendship Hall was recently restored by Dr. M. Fred Tidwell and Joseph B. Gavlick. It was included in the National Register of Historic Places in 1973.

GLASGOW

1500 Hambrooks Boulevard, Cambridge

In Cambridge, on the boulevard forming the western boundary of the city, is Glasgow, ancestral seat of the Tubman family. This lovely home, with its beautiful lawns and gardens, fronts on the Great Choptank and lies half a mile from the river.

In 1760 there came to Maryland William Murray, ward of the Clan Murray in Scotland, who purchased the tract of land known as "Ayreshire" and renamed it "Glasgow" after his native city. In that same year the present Colonial mansion was built.

The two-and-a-half storey part of the house has massive walls of English brick painted white, while the one-and-a-half storey wing built in 1881 is covered with white clapboard. Three brick chimneys rise from the roof. A simple floor of brick lies before the front door, but there is a large modern porch on the left of the house.

In order that the landing of the stairs might not be seen, the decoration over the panelled front door is of wood rather than the customary glass. The front door opens on a hall with the stairway on the right rising in two flights to the upper storeys. At the foot of the stairs on the left is the door to the living room. Further down the hall on the same side is the door to the drawing room. Both these rooms, which give on the porch, are wainscoted to three feet and have fireplaces. The hall is also wainscoted and has a fine carved arch dividing it into two parts. The large garden door is panelled on the outside and diagonally battened inside. The dining room is entered by a door on the right of the hall. This chamber is delightfully proportioned and panelled to the ceiling. From it doors open into the kitchen and a hall with a flight of stairs to the servants' quarters. A pantry lies beyond.

Glasgow has an air of permanence, as though it would stand even after the face of the land surrounding it had changed. Indeed, the very partition walls in the house are of brick.

The first Murray had a famous grandson, William Vans Murray, who was Minister to Holland, and, in 1800, one of the negotiators of the treaty with France. He served in the second, third, and fourth Congress and died at the height of his career, in 1803, when he was only forty-one years of age. His sister, Henrietta Murray, inherited Glasgow. She was married to Dr. George I. Robertson, who sold the property, then composed of four hundred twenty-nine and one-half acres, to Dr. Robert F. Tubman, on July 14, 1842.

Dr. Tubman was born at St. Giles Fields, May 7, 1791. He graduated from the University of Pennsylvania and started practicing at Medicine Hall, now known as Golden Hill. This well-beloved doctor died Christmas Eve, 1864, willing Glasgow to his youngest son, Robert Constantine Tubman, who lived there until his death in 1916. His son and heir, Robert E. Tubman, made extensive researches into the history of both Glasgow and his own family, as he was interested in preserving as much as possible of old Maryland in these hurried and thoughtless times. After his death in 1938, Glasgow remained in the Tubman family another 10 years. It has since been owned by the Glovers, and then the Barnes family, who purchased it in 1970. In 1983, they were planning to sell Glasgow.

BENNETT'S ADVENTURE

Clifford Cooper Road, Allen

On the north side of Wicomico Creek, about one mile from its opening into Wicomico River, stands a large dwelling set among a grove of old trees. Built between 1730 and 1740 by Colonel George Dashiell, the house is the largest gambrel-roofed dwelling in the area.

In 1665, Major Richard Bennett patented a tract of twenty five hundred acres. In 1721, George Dashiell bought the land from one of Bennett's grandchildren and had it resurveyed and patented for seventeen hundred forty acres. Dashiell was a wealthy planter and a member of the Lower House of the Assembly. Colonel John Stewart, who fought in the Revolutionary War, acquired it in 1791.

One-and-a-half storeys high, the building is laid in Flemish bond with a string course at roofline and a moulded water table at the base. The house is rectangular, with pairs of interlocking diamonds of purple, glazed brick headers set between the four front and rear windows and on each gable end. Three pointed dormers extend over the wall line providing light for the quaintly shaped bedrooms. The entrance steps to the wide and commodious cellar are covered by a magnificent entrance arch supporting the chimney stack and fireplace. On each side of the fireplace, on the west end, a small window punctuates the exterior.

The front door is shaded by a small porch and opens into a wide center hall. The hall, flat panelled from floor to ceiling on both sides, leads to spacious rooms on either side of it with their entrance doors being to the front and rear of the hall. Entering the hall from the creek side (the main entrance) the stairway lies to the right and beyond the entrance to the room on the right.

The Great Room, situated to the left, is a spacious 20′ × 24′, has a high ceiling, and two large windows—one facing north, the other, south. Raised panels cover the west wall from ceiling to floor. Pilasters flank the fireplace. On each side of the fireplace is a closet—each lighted by a small window. The hall side is also panelled to the ceiling. Cornices put the finishing touch on the Great Room.

There is little room at the head of the stair. However, two doors open to bedrooms on either side—one faces the land; the other, the creek.

The east end has a modern addition dated from 1948 containing features of contemporary life; not in character with the original house.

Bennett's Adventure has been known by a number of different names through the course of history, including Dashiell's Lot, Paul Jones House, Westfield and Bryan's Manor.

NEW NITHSDALE

Pemberton Drive, Salisbury

On a bluff facing south over the Wicomico River sits New Nithsdale, about four miles downstream from Salisbury with Rockawalkin Creek on its west side. The brick house has one-and-a-half storeys, three dormers on the front facade, and two inside chimneys. One of the most remarkable features is the glaze on the bricks. The purple headers blaze in the sun like deep amethysts, and the pale salmon bricks provide a background which makes this house gleam like a Byzantine mosaic. The two windows in the front and back are capped with rubbed brick flat arches.

Many original features are still evident in the house. The front entrance has a five-panelled front door under a three-light transom. All the interior doors are handworked, handpegged and five panelled. The stairway is simple in design with two square balusters on each step, a rounded handrail, and square newel posts and caps.

The east room, to the right of the central hall, contains a very large restored pale salmon brick fireplace, topped with arched headers. The west room has the original split laths, shell and horsehair plaster walls, and a smaller fireplace flanked by two closets.

On the second floor, the west bedroom has two closets hidden behind a complete wall of handcarved panelling with a small fireplace inserted. The original handwork is also displayed in the doors and wide plank flooring.

Not far from the house is a small cemetery with more than a dozen 19th century grave markers with names of the McBryde, Hooper and Slemonds families.

Levin Gale purchased the property in 1731 and built the house. Levin was the son of George Gale, an early trader. The younger Gale was one of five commissioners appointed by the Maryland Assembly to establish Princess Anne in 1733.

According to tradition, on one of Captain Levin Gale's many trips, he sailed into Bermuda to obtain food and water. He found the natives in revolt, and a family engaged him to take them away from the island. That night their baggage went aboard accompanied by a boy of four and a girl of six. The children knew their names only as John and Frances, but the name *North* appeared on a trunk and in some books. The parents failed to board, and Captain Gale was finally forced by a threatened attack to sail without them. He took the children home to his new house in Maryland.

At the first opportunity, he returned to Bermuda but could find no trace of anybody belonging to the children. So John and Frances North grew up in their foster father's house. John was lost at sea as a young man, and Frances married Captain William Murray, a Scottish seaman who named this house after his native Nithsdale. From them descended William Murray Stone, who became the third Episcopal Bishop of Maryland in 1830.

In 1886 John Oscar Freeney inherited the farm. It is said that Mr. Freeney married a lady from Baltimore who was so homesick that she spent all her time looking out the windows toward her native city. Her husband stood this as long as he could, and then had the windows removed in order to stop her staring. In proof of this, all the windows on the western side of the house have been bricked up.

In 1956 the restoration and an addition were completed by Otis G. and Elizabeth Richardson Esham, and they are the residing owners.

PEMBERTON HALL

Pemberton Drive, Salisbury

Pemberton Hall, located three miles southwest of Salisbury, stands on a rise a few hundred yards from the Wicomico River. The Pemberton Hall tract, first patented in 1679 to William Stevens, was transferred to Thomas Pemberton four years later. In 1726, Joseph Pemberton sold the land to Isaac Handy, the builder of Pemberton Hall. According to tradition, Loyalists gathered at Pemberton Hall during the American Revolution.

The Handy family played significant roles in the affairs of the state. Isaac Handy, who built the Hall in 1741, was a Justice of the Peace, a planter, and a colonel in the Maryland militia. After Isaac's death in 1763, Pemberton became the property of his son, Henry. Another of Isaac's sons, George, served in the Maryland Line in the Fifth Regiment as well as Lee's Dragoons in the American Revolution. Isaac's granddaughter, Frances, married a hero in the American Revolution, Alexander Roxbury. Another of his descendents, William Handy earned distinction as a Maryland state legislator.

In 1868, at a trustees' sale, James Cannon and Elihu Jackson bought Pemberton Hall. Cannon owned the building itself and the land surrounding it. Jackson went on to become Governor of Maryland. In 1884, Cannon sold his interest in Pemberton Hall to Cadmus J. Taylor, who willed the property to his son, James. James Taylor's son, Rex Taylor, a judge of the Wicomico County Circuit Court, and his brother, Seth Taylor, owned Pemberton Hall until 1963, at which time the Foundation took it over.

This one-and-a-half storey brick house has a gambrel roof and three hipped-roof dormers on each side. The brick is laid in Flemish bond. The central doors are double and have four panels in each door. Above the door and windows are flat gauged brick arches. "1741" is scratched in a brick above the side door. Two chimneys, one at either end of the house, project from the main structure.

The interior has a large square hall with raised panelling on two sides. The fireplace wall and chimney breast are decorated with pilasters, and there is an enclosed staircase to both the second floor and into the basement. On the south side of the fireplace, a cupboard is no longer there. Beyond this hall room are two smaller rooms, each with a panelled chimney piece. The second floor is divided into a hall and four bedrooms. In the southeast bedroom is an unusual valance board made to hold the curtains of a low post bed.

Pemberton Hall, with its wide curved eaves and sparkling glazed brick, composes a picture reminiscent of rural England.

POPLAR HILL MANSION

117 Elizabeth Street, Salisbury

Situated on the highest rise in Salisbury, facing down Poplar Hill Avenue, is Poplar Hill Mansion. Built in 1810, this home is an example of Federal architecture. Interestingly, the mansion is also reminiscent of the New England architecture of the period.

Major Levin Handy was the first owner of Poplar Hill. He ventured to Maryland from Rhode Island in the late eighteenth century. Handy, a man of wealth, had the finest materials used in the construction of his home, including New Jersey heart pine.

The building is two storeys high. Under the high pitched roof is a large attic, lit by two windows, east and west. In addition, a loft is lit by bull's eye windows in each gable end. Two chimneys rise 15 feet above the roof.

A large panelled door with fan light above accents the door opening. Column pilasters flank the door, as well. On each side are two large 12/12 paned windows.

Inside, above the stair, a handsome Palladian window lights the front hall. A similar window provides light at the rear stair landing. The wide hall has an accenting interior arch. A stairway rises on the right behind the arch. To the right of the front hall is the east chamber with two windows on the front facade and three on the east. A fireplace with a mantel shelf sits on the left wall. A doorway on the right leads to the rear hall and back stair. Notable architectural features of the room include flat panelled dado with carving and cornices.

To the left of the front hall is a parlor with a fireplace and two windows, west and south. This room also has panelled dado, carved decoration, and cornices. To the left of the fireplace is a passage leading along the chimney stack to the rear sitting room. This room holds a fireplace and two windows. It is finished in a much simpler manner. Originally, the woodwork in the front hall and east room was marbleized. The rear hall has an exterior door under the stairway leading to a piazza.

The second floor plan duplicates that of the first floor. Rooms are finished with chair rails and cornices, though plainer than those found downstairs.

There is a full basement under the house with a floor plan similar to the two levels above. Original batten doors, wooden locks, and wood strap hinges remain, along with barred windows. The entrance sits under the rear piazza.

Poplar Hill Mansion has had many owners since Major Levin Handy. The property currently belongs to the City of Salisbury, and is a National Trust house.

BEVERLY FARM

Route 13, Princess Anne

On the south side of Kings Creek is Beverly Farm. This beautiful old two-and-a-half storey Georgian house was finished in 1796, according to the date on the chimney. Its facade, broken by dormer windows, rises in conscious dignity from surrounding shrubbery, suggesting an English country house of the late eighteenth century.

Beverly Farm was built by Nehemiah King II, who died June 12, 1802, three years before his fiftieth birthday. His daughter, Laura King, married Isaac T. Barnes, overseer of the farm. The estate was purchased from their heirs by Lynde Catlin of New York in 1906. Mr. Catlin and his wife took great pride in their home and spent a great deal of time and money restoring it until it became one of the show places of the Eastern Shore. In 1936 William Perry bought the mansion for a summer home.

In 1937 the main block of Beverly suffered a severe fire set by a disgruntled former employee. Through the good fortune of having excellent photographic documentation of the pre-fire interior and the financial ability to undertake the task, Mr. Perry painstakingly restored the house. Wherever possible, original material was reused in the restoration though the fire had left little standing but the exterior walls. It was during this restoration that the original parlor became the dining room which had been located in the wing prior to the fire. As a result of damage to the exterior, the brick was sprayed with concrete and painted.

The house passed from the Perry family in 1953 to the Babcock family who owned it until 1967 when it was purchased by Francis L. Hayman. A second tragic fire in 1977 destroyed the wing on the northwest side of the house which predated the main block. The exterior of the wing was reconstructed according to photographs of the original structure and an appropriate interior was designed for use as office and living quarters.

The house's front facade is broken by a two storey bay. The front door, flanked by windows, opens into the twelve foot wide hall. This bisects the main building, on the left side of which is the door to a large square living room where there is a chair rail and a large elaborately decorated mantel-piece. On the right of the hall is the door to the large dining room. Four large windows make the lofty room light and airy.

The stair hall is at right angles to the main hall and is entered through a separate door. Opposite is the door to a small library. A frame kitchen wing connecting the main part of the house to the earlier brick-end wing was added during the early twentieth century.

The course of history was very nearly altered at Beverly Farm when Jerome Bonaparte was in America, for he became a close friend of Robert Jenkins Henry King—so much so that the two contemplated rescuing Napoleon from St. Helena. They had constructed behind the fireplace of the second floor front bedroom a secret room entered by what seemed to be a small wood closet, in which the Emperor was to be concealed. A schooner was hired and held in readiness for the completion of plans which had to be made in Europe. Just before the ship was about to sail from Cape Charles, word was received from France that the Emperor was dead.

This great mansion was constructed of materials gathered from the surrounding land. The bricks were made on the estate, and oyster shells were burned to produce lime. On the interior thick plaster was applied directly to the bricks. All through the house the floor boards are of heart pine one and three-quarter inches thick and laid transversely. The stairs are of black walnut built with such care it is quite possible to see why almost two decades passed before completion of the building.

BRENTWOOD FARM

Allen Road, Princess Anne

In 1738, the Reverend Alexander Adams, first rector of Stepney Parish, Somerset County, built himself a brick house on the banks of Wicomico Creek, just one hundred feet from the water. He named it Adams' Adventure. After Mr. Adams died the house passed to another family, and some time before 1806 the records show that for reasons unknown the dwelling was then called End of Strife. In 1806, when a deed involving the place was made, the present name, Brentwood Farm, was applied and it is by this title that the house has been known since then.

In 1901 Dr. George W. Jarman bought Brentwood Farm from a Mrs. Robinson and carried out extensive additions and alterations, keeping to spirit of the house and making few changes in the interior arrangements. There was a quaint circular staircase in the right end of the hall, so small and narrow that it was difficult to use. Time had made it unsafe, so this stair was removed, and at the same time a number of the termite-eaten original wide boards were replaced by less antique but more practical flooring. During the alterations a boxed-in log stairway to the attic had to be taken out. On one of its steps were carved initials and the year by which we date the building of the house.

The present front door is a modern one but beautifully designed. It opens on a wide hall which runs parallel to the long facade of the house, a feature which is seldom found in Maryland dwellings. At one end of this is a porch and at the other the door into the large wing. A wide opening opposite the front door gives on the library. Here there is a corner fireplace with panelling of extremely wide boards to the ceiling, and no mantel. A fine corner cupboard graces another corner of the room. There were originally two rooms to the right of this, each containing a corner fireplace, but the partition was taken out, and a single fireplace and mantel were substituted. Today this room is used as a living room.

Many of the old Maryland homes have their secrets, but few as fascinating as the curious underground room which was to the right of Brentwood Farm. This was about fifteen feet deep and ten feet wide with a very narrow approach. It has been suggested that this was a retreat from Indians, as it could easily be defended. However, the truth of the matter will never be known as the cave has been covered up by the new wing.

Today Brentwood Farm serenely rests encircled by its trees and beautiful grounds, a worthy setting for one of the most pleasant old homes of Maryland. Its mellow brick walls and twinkling windows are a delight to the visitor who is sure to receive a kindly welcome from Judge and Mrs. E. McMaster Duer.

KINGSTON HALL

Route 667, Westover

Kingston Hall sits at the headwaters of the Annemessex River, one-half mile from the town of Kingston in Somerset County. It is a small late-eighteenth century house with interesting architectural features. The room arrangement with its corner fireplaces and corner hall reflects the traditional plan common to the early decades of the century. Its exterior detail, specifically the window treatment and the pedimented pavilion with circular gable window, is indicative of mid-Georgian style. The woodwork and mantels in some rooms suggest a transitional style from late Georgian into Federal.

Kingston Hall's history began in the mid-eighteenth century when Robert King owned the property. The King family were large land owners at that time. Robert's son, Nehemiah, built Beverly of Somerset, and it was his grandson, Thomas King, who erected Kingston Hall. Thomas King had inherited the tract of land located on an 860 acre plantation. Also on the property: King's "Dwelling House," kitchen, dairy house, smoke house, stable, hen house, three corn houses, a granary, "a Negro house," blacksmith's shop, two barns and three log houses. Interestingly, Thomas King grew grain, not tobacco, which was the crop most commonly associated with eighteenth century tidewater culture.

When Thomas King died around the turn of the nineteenth century, King's daughter and son-in-law Henry James Carroll assumed ownership of Kingston Hall. Their son, Thomas King Carroll, inherited the property in 1818. His daughter, Anna Ella Carroll, born at the house in 1815, became a national figure as an unofficial advisor to Abraham Lincoln. Anna Carroll also planned a land seige of Vicksburg which effected the town's surrender in 1863. Thomas King Carroll attained prominence, as well, though his notoriety was only statewide. Carroll served as delegate, judge, and later as Governor of Maryland. During his year as Governor, Carroll encouraged the improvement of the University of Maryland, advocated penal reform, and earned the reputation as a politician who dispensed patronage freely.

In the 1820's, the Circuit Court of Somerset County decreed that Carroll had accumulated outstanding debts to a man named William Williams. Then, in 1835, the court authorized the sale of Kingston Hall to cover Carroll's debts. The new owner, John Upshur Dennis, introduced another political family to Kingston Hall. Three members of the family served in the House of Representatives. Dennis' son, George Robertson Dennis, who inherited Kingston Hall in 1851, served in the House of Delegates and the Senate. He ran for governor unsuccessfully in 1879 and terminated his political career soon after, retiring to Kingston Hall. During the twentieth century, the property has had many owners, and the current ones are Dr. and Mrs. J. Richard Warbasse.

All brick, Kingston Hall is composed of a large two-storey section connected by a passageway to a smaller two-storey wing. The Flemish bond brickwork is painted white. There are inside end chimneys on both the east and west gables.

The front door to the main section of Kingston Hall opens into a large wainscoted hall. The stairs rise on the opposite wall, starting at the far right, and are panelled. In line with the front door is the door to the living room with its fine corner fireplace and panelling from floor to ceiling. This is the only room of the fourteen in the house so decorated. There are two other rooms parallel with the hall and living room and each has a corner fireplace. All of the windows in the main section are splayed.

The great kitchen of Kingston Hall is connected to the main building by a passageway off of which a modern bathroom has been built. The kitchen has a huge fireplace, eight feet long, four feet high, and three feet deep, with the original iron crane still hanging in it.

TEACKLE MANSION

Prince William Street, Princess Anne

At the head waters of the Manokin River is the town of Princess Anne, charming and hospitable in the best tradition of the Eastern Shore. Its streets are shaded by venerable trees. The Washington Hotel, famed Revolutionary War hostelry, still looks much the same as it did when Luther Martin, first Attorney-General of the State of Maryland; Governor Thomas King Carroll; Governor Levin Winder; Judge Samuel Chase; and a host of other distinguished men visited its friendly halls. On the outskirts of Princess Anne stands Teackle Mansion, erected by Littleton Dennis Teackle on part of "Beckford" estate, which was patented to Edmund Howard in 1681. The owner, a prominent man in Somerset County, was founder and first president of the Bank of Somerset, the earliest banking institution in the county, a member of the Maryland Assembly, and an important figure in our trade with England.

The design of the building was the result of a trip Mr. Teackle made to Glasgow, Scotland, where he saw a fine old castle. Delighted with its appearance, he determined to build himself a house in Maryland as much like the castle as he could manage.

Teackle Mansion has a two-hundred foot facade divided into two wings connected to the central section by large two storey passageways. Although outwardly there is not much similarity in appearance between Teackle Mansion and Doughoregan Manor in Howard County, the general plan is much the same. Both are long, rather low, and not very wide, with the connecting sections only one room in width.

The whole building is of brick with a cellar under the central section only. An interesting feature of the house is the rectangular sunken panels filled with plaster placed over each first storey window in place of the usual string course. Curiously enough this architectural departure seems to be limited to an area near Princess Anne. Other houses similarly decorated are Beckford, built in 1776 by Henry Jackson on the same estate, and the Robertson House.

The building of Teackle Mansion was begun in 1801 with the central section of the house; the two wings and passageways were put up a year apart, the mansion taking three years to finish. Not satisfied with having one of the most imposing establishments in the country, Mr. Teackle planted an extensive garden running to the banks of the Manokin River. In fact he spent so much money on his home that he was impoverished, and when the trustees settled the estate, Teackle Mansion had to be sold.

Dr. John Dashiell purchased the property from the trustees in 1852. It was divided into three parts, even to the house itself, and now there are three separate sections of the building, each with an individual deed.

The southern and middle sections are now owned by Olde Princess Anne Days, Inc., and the northern section by the Somerset County Historical Society. The mansion is usually open on Sundays or by appointment.

BEVERLY

Cedar Hill Wharf Road, Pocomoke City

Beverly lies a mile from the Virginia border on the east bank of the Pocomoke River, approximately six miles southwest of Pocomoke City. Built in 1774, Beverly is a fine example of Colonial architecture, Georgian style. The size and elegance of this mansion reflect the prominent position its builders held in Worcester County. It is larger and more formal than most houses of the period in southeastern Maryland.

Littleton Dennis, a successful lawyer, began construction of Beverly in the late 1760's to early 1770's. When he died in 1774, his wife, Susanna Upshur Dennis, had the house completed. At that time, ownership fell to Littleton's son, John; Susanna became executor of the estate. An inventory of Littleton Dennis's possessions showed him to be an extremely wealthy man. In addition to Beverly, he owned four other properties and many slaves.

John Dennis, son of Littleton and Susanna, was a member of Congress for ten years. In 1800, he was one of the five Federalist Congressmen to change a vote from Aaron Burr to Thomas Jefferson to break the deadlock in the Presidential election. In 1798, Dennis had several tracts of his land resurveyed and later patented as "Dennis's Union." Four years later, John sold most of this land to his brother, Littleton Dennis, a lawyer and Worcester County Judge of Appeals. Littleton's 1831 bequest deeded Beverly to his sons, Littleton Upshur Dennis and John Upshur Dennis. Littleton died a few years after his father and John took sole possession of the property at that time. John Upshur Dennis was a successful planter and merchant who owned a large amount of property like his grandfather, Littleton. At his death, John Upshur Dennis left the estate to two of his sons, Samuel King Dennis and Arthur Emerson Dennis. Samuel King Dennis, who was a member of the Maryland legislature for a time, deeded Beverly to his five sons, several of whom were also active in state law and politics, around the turn of the century. In 1927, Beverly was sold out of the Dennis family. Mr. and Mrs. John Butler now own Beverly.

Beverly is five bays wide and three deep. It is two storeys plus an attic. The rose-colored brick is laid in Flemish bond above and below the moulded water table. There is a central door on the river facades surmounted by a small, heavy fanlight with a gauged brick arch. On each bay, first and second storeys, is a 12/12 window. The flat arches above the windows are also gauged brick. A heavy modillion cornice with dentil frieze sits along the roof. Especially notable are the wrought iron railings and a delicate arch that lead up the steps to the main door. A two-storey pedimented portico with fluted Greek ionic columns covers the three center bays of the east facade. Chimneys extend above the north and south ends.

Extending from the center and east bays is a one-storey hyphen of beaded clapboard. Another beaded clapboard wing adjoining Beverly on the south end is two storeys.

There are six rooms on the first floor of the mansion. The northwest room is completely panelled. A fireplace, centered on the north wall, is surrounded by a black marble architrave, in the middle of which is a white marble keystone. Fluted pilasters with full entablature frame the chimney breast. The room has a heavy cornice with dentil moulding and a bolection chair rail.

The parlor is much less elaborate. The fireplace wall is fully panelled. Flanked by two closets, the fireplace itself is framed by fluted pilasters. The center tablet has an Adamesque sunburst. The room has a simple cornice and panelled wainscot.

The graceful, scrolled two-run stairway in the west hall has three block and turn balusters per tread. Four balusters form the column at the bottom of the stairway. The step ends are scrolled.

A small southwest room has a panelled wainscot and simple cornice. It also has a corner fireplace with a simple architrave and mantel shelf.

The dining room, or southeast room, has a fireplace, a simple cornice, panelled wainscot and window recesses. An eight-panel door leads into the hyphen containing a modern kitchen.

CHANCEFORD

209 West Federal Street, Snow Hill

In Snow Hill, almost in the center of Worcester County on the Eastern Shore, stands Chanceford or Ingleside. This large two-and-a-half storey Colonial house is a little removed from the street, with its white stuccoed brick walls withdrawn from stir and bustle.

The house is supposed to have been built in 1793, immediately after the property was purchased from Francis Ross by James Rounds Morris, Clerk of the Court of Worcester County. No record is found of the date when the building was erected.

Chanceford's front door is in the pedimented gable-end of the building which would usually be the side. The gable-end has a full pediment with dentils and modillions, and a bull's-eye window with a star pattern in the center. Below this round window are three small rectangular windows, an arrangement unusual in Maryland. An exterior panelled door has been added outside of the original door to protect it from the weather. A shallow overhang roof conforms to the shape of the house roof with similar dentils and is supported by columns which flank the doorway.

The doors of Chanceford are of two-ply thickness with inner sides diagonally laid. There are also stout wooden bars and large wooden locks, H and HL hinges, all through the house. The front door has a heart-and-star leaded transom over it, and opens into the hall running the length of the house. Immediately on the right are the mahogany-railed stairs. Doors to the fifteen by seventeen foot living room and fifteen by sixteen foot other living room open off the hall. Each has a large fireplace with well designed mantels.

At one time detached from the main structure, the former ballroom, twenty by twenty-two feet, was subsequently joined to the larger wing by an addition, now used as the dining room. The former ballroom, now a kitchen and breakfast room, has its own staircase which has square reeded balusters, panelling, and intricate step-ends. The mantel of the former ballroom was moved into the dining room, where there is an operating fireplace. There is a three foot wainscoting about the room and fluted panels under the windows. In 1971, a solarium was added to the rear of the house, off the present kitchen. This is connected by a breezeway to the garage and shop.

The second owner of Chanceford was Judge William Whittington, who died there in 1827 and is buried nearby. His son-in-law, Judge William Tingle, inherited. In 1916 the house was in the possession of Mrs. Eugene Riggin of Los Angeles, California, and was later owned by John W. Stanton of Snow Hill. The current owner is Judge Edward O. Thomas. It is probably not coincidence that several members of the judiciary have owned Chanceford, since both the Worcester County Court House and the District Court are also located in Snow Hill, only a few blocks from this stately home.

The once extensive garden has been reduced to a few clumps of boxwood, but the fine old English ivy which tradition says was brought from Kenilworth Castle is still green. Chanceford has been well preserved through the years and is an excellent example of a Colonial dwelling in which a classic exterior is combined with a large and comfortable interior.

FASSITT HOUSE

Route 611, Berlin

Four and a half miles southwest of Berlin facing Sinepuxent Bay, stands the small one-and-a-half storey brick building known as Fassitt House. It was built by the family of the same name around 1669. The family was prominent in the early 1700's, as Judge Fassitt had jurisdiction in the area which currently comprises both Worcester and Wicomico counties.

The house is forty by twenty-four feet and is built entirely of brick. It has one brick chimney but from the evidence of new brick in the south wall probably another fireplace was there at one time. The exterior walls are most interesting, as they are decorated with remarkable glazed diamond and herringbone designs. It has been said the Colonial builder liked to give his love of color and vivid display free rein in gay and complicated brick work. Fassitt House is the best example of this in Maryland. Another interesting feature is the presence of six large windows, with at least one at each cardinal point of the compass. Thus, the sun shines in Fassitt House from sunrise to sunset each day.

Many of the homes in the neighborhood display the same architectural characteristics, so much so that it seems that one man, long forgotten, must have designed them all. Like the names of almost all Colonial architects, his has not survived. Of course, the owner often planned his dwelling himself. There is a story concerning the gentleman who designed Rich Hall, since burned, near Port Tobacco in Charles County. He instructed the carpenter to proceed exactly according to his plans. When the home was finished, the amateur architect viewed it with pride, only to discover to his chagrin that he had neglected to include a stairway to the second floor.

However, Fassitt House did not suffer in this respect as it has a well constructed flight of stairs in its own hall opening into the main hall bisecting the house. The stairway has a "duck" newel, so called because of the curious curve in the newel head. The original handrail is still intact. A commodious closet opens off the first landing. The largest room in the house is the living room, which is entered on the right of the hall. The dining room door is almost opposite and it is from this room that the corner fireplace was removed.

In the War of 1812 Fassitt House was fired upon by the British fleet, but the inhabitants had left, after burying the family silver. Much of the original silverware, as well as the oriental rugs, are still found within the home.

Fassitt House is still owned by descendants of the original family, Mrs. Margaret R. Carey and her son, Edward Fassitt Carey. Mrs. Carey and her late husband, Edward Lee Carey, restored Fassitt House in 1950 and moved there in 1951. They hosted an open house that Christmas for over 600 guests, including noted historian Henry Chandlee Forman. All of the original panelling and pine floors remain, and the only new part of the house is the huge kitchen and porch. Mr. Carey cut a compass in the inlaid kitchen floor, so guests could tell from what direction the sun was shining.

Edward Lee Carey's great-grandfather, Joshua Carey, married into the Fassitt family to begin the Carey line of ownership. His father, Edward James Carey, was captain of the police boats for Baltimore Harbor, while Edward Lee Carey was the first paid captain of the Ocean City Beach Patrol.

GENEZAR

Route 611, Berlin

Eight miles from Berlin, on the Sinepuxent Neck, stands Genezar, a tall narrow house rising sheer from the ground. Originally there must have been shrubbery, but today nothing hides the meeting of bricks and sod. The complicated pattern of the brick work reveals that it was built at a time when bricklaying was an art. Today this house is beginning to show signs of age with a brick missing here and there.

Major John Purnell, who married the daughter of Littleton Robins, related by marriage to Oliver Cromwell, built Genezar in 1732 and it stands, with the exception of one wall, unchanged by time or man. Although not a large mansion, such as Tulip Hill or Readbourne, it was the home of cultured people for many generations.

When Major Purnell died, the property passed to his daughter, who married John P. Marshall. Again a daughter inherited, and became the wife of Robert Jenkins Henry. Since then it has passed from father to son in the Henry family, being owned successively by Major Edward Henry; by Zadok P. Henry, who inherited in 1868; by his son, Zadok P. Henry; and by his son, Dr. Zadok P. Henry, a prominent citizen of Berlin. It was later owned by Mr. and Mrs. Donald Humphrey. Since 1974, the entire estate, on both sides of Route 611, has belonged to the G.P. Limited Partnership. The property on the east side of the road has been developed, while the house itself and about 200 acres of land remain in its original setting.

The whole house seems to have been constructed at one time. A large chimney rises at either end of the main section, and a small chimney from the wing. In order to preserve the bricks a coat of whitewash was applied up to the eaves. It has faded until the dominant colors are soft grey and green. The fine modillion cornice has dentils and wave bed moulds, above which a single narrow pointed dormer looks to the north.

The facade is charmingly irregular, although it is hard to judge its original proportions without the small porch, which has been removed. A single step leads to the hall, running the depth of the house. The front is pierced by another door opening into the middle section, where the back wall is of frame construction.

The front hall, panelled to the chair rail, has steps unguarded by banisters leading to the second storey. All the doors are under six feet in height. On the left as one enters is the door to the living room. This, as well as the dining room directly across from it, has a ceiling of broad brown planks. In the parlor a chair rail runs about the room while a wooden cornice joins the wall and ceiling; the mantel-piece is decorated with elaborate mouldings. Above this room is a bedroom panelled in squares from floor to ceiling. The dining room has a three foot wainscoting and a built-in corner cupboard with a curved shell top and butterfly shelves.

The homes in this book which have been designated on the National Register of Historic Places appear below. The name of the home is followed by the month and year it was entered on the Register. The homes are listed in the order in which they were entered.

Hammond-Harwood House	October, 1960	Bohemia	April, 1973
Whitehall	October, 1960	Tudor Hall	April, 1973
Hampton National Historic Site	July, 1968	Medical Hall	August, 1973
Chase-Lloyd House	April, 1970	Sophia's Dairy	September, 1973
Montpelier	April, 1970	Friendship Hall	October, 1973
Brice House	May, 1970	Clifton	June, 1974
Mount Clare Mansion	May, 1970	Myrtle Grove	August, 1974
Tulip Hill	May, 1970	Snow Hill	August, 1974
Wye House	May, 1970	Preston-on-Patuxent	October, 1974
Shriver House (Union Mills Homestead)	January, 1971	Hager's Choice	November, 1974
Pemberton Hall	February, 1971	Kingston Hall	December, 1974
Genezar	September, 1971	St. Paul's Rectory	March, 1975
Poplar Hill Mansion	October, 1971	Oak Lawn	May, 1975
Teackle Mansion	October, 1971	Hinchingham	September, 1975
Doughoregan Manor	November, 1971	Beverly (Worcester)	October, 1975
Rose Hill Manor	December, 1971	Bennett's Adventure	November, 1975
Godlington Manor	February, 1972	Glasgow	October, 1976
Homewood	February, 1972	Bard's Fields	November, 1976
Cedar Park	April, 1972	Belair	September, 1977
Michael Cresap House	April, 1972	Bon Air	November, 1977
Habre de Venture	October, 1972	Long Meadows	September, 1978
Widehall	October, 1972	Fat Oxen	May, 1979
Batchelor's Hope	November, 1972	Octorara	May, 1980
Sotterley	November, 1972	Otwell	March, 1982
Paca House and Garden	February, 1973	Burleigh Manor	November, 1982
Mulberry Fields	March, 1973	Potter Hall	November, 1982
Beverly (Somerset)	March, 1973	Kennersley	May, 1983

ACKNOWLEDGEMENTS

The author and publisher wish to thank the following for their contributions to the updating of the 1939 limited edition and their efforts in achieving historical accuracy.

Rodney Little, Peter Kurtze, Orlando Ridout IV and Miriam Hensley of the Maryland Historical Trust, for opening their files for the research effort.

General Orwin Talbott and Polly Barber of the Maryland Heritage Committee.

Arthur F. Ballant, Jr. for his editorial and layout direction and exhaustive research.

Lynn Ritter and Patricia Grutkowski for their editorial efforts in rewriting individual home descriptions.

Finally, to the owners and interested citizens of Maryland who aided the research effort by providing vital information:

Rev. Irving Allen, Hope Andrews, Shirley V. Baltz, Mrs. Gordon Barnes, Michael Bourne, Rhoda E. Bowers, Barbara A. Brand, Eveleth W. Bridgeman, Jr., Elizabeth Bullard, Margaret R. Carey, John L. Carnochan, Jr., O. Raymond Carrington, Philip Carroll, Martha C. Carter, Pamela Charshee, Judy Cheseldine, David Clark, Edith D. Connolly, Warren J. Cox, Dr. John H. Cumberland, Milton Dance, W.M. Darden, Nancy Dick, Dr. Norton T. Dodge, Judge E. McMaster Duer, Dwight Early, Elizabeth R. Esham, Thomas T. Firth, Jr., A.J. Fletcher, John Flewelling, Mrs. Mary Force, Hope H. Grace, Mrs. Montgomery Meigs Green, Lynne Dakin Hastings, Louise L. Hayman, Elizabeth Hill, Alen Hollomon, Barbara and Errol Houck, Arthur A. Houghton, Jr., Wilbur Ross Hubbard, Phyllis Hurd, Mabel Satterlee Ingalls, Elmer M. Jackson, Jr., Sue M. Jackson, Mary Lennox Jansson, Rev. Edward J. Kaczorowski, William G. Kerbin, Jr., G. Rex Kilbourn, Jr., Dorothy Morton Kimberly, John E. King, Rita Knox, Allen Kotras, Dr. Sidney D. Kreider, Janet Lybarger, Dr. Monroe H. Martin, Don Mastroni, John W. McGrain, W. Harrison Mechling, Andrew J. Michael, Calvin W. Mowbray, Ann E. Moylan, Jim Nelson, Arthur G. Nichols, Jr., Peter Nyce, Phylis Reeve O'Connor, Franklin B. Olmsted, Gordon O'Neill, James Pratt, Judith Profitt, Dorothy T. Rainwater, Mrs. Thomas Rankin, Mr. and Mrs. Eugene Rea, Dick Revie, Nancy G. Richards, Eugenie LeMerle Riggs, Mrs. Lou Rose, Samuel G. Rose, Charles Scarlett, Jr., Mark N. Schatz, Elizabeth Lloyd Schiller, Esther L. Shriver, Elizabeth S. Simpson, Hugh Smith, Mary Miller Strauss, C. John Sullivan, Jane C. Sween, Pringle Symonds, Judge Edward O. Thomas, Dr. M. Fred Tidwell, Anton J. Urbas, Mrs. Bryan P. Warren, Charles E. Wegner, C. Robert Withey, Charles Yaeger, Gale H. Yerges, and the staffs of Historic Annapolis, Inc., the Naval Academy Alumni Association and St. Paul's Rectory.

INDEX

The original edition of *Colonial and Historic Homes of Maryland*, published in 1939, was a collaboration of Baltimorean S. Donovan Swann, Sr., and his son, S. Donovan Swann, Jr. For four years, father and son researched the project; the Swanns spent three of those years in the field. The elder Swann created the etchings, while Don, Jr., provided the descriptions of over one hundred homes.

The late Don Swann, Sr., completed more than six hundred etchings over a period of twenty-five years. His work has been exhibited throughout the United States and is in the permanent collections of the Metropolitan Museum, the Smithsonian Institution, and the Library of Congress. Mr. Swann was a graduate of St. John's College in Annapolis, served as a flyer in World War I and a public relations officer in World War II. For a time, he managed the Baltimore Opera Company. He was also an accomplished musician and inventor, as well as golf champ. Married to Margarita Swann, Don Swann, Sr., was the father of three children, Don, Jr., Frances, and Lynn.

Don Swann, Jr., born in Baltimore in 1911, attended St. Paul's School, Gilman School, and was graduated from Princeton University in 1934. For two years, he did graduate study at the Johns Hopkins University before serving as a Captain in the Army. He then spent twenty-two years managing the first professional summer theater in Maryland, the Hilltop Theater, and since 1954, has been president of the Etchcrafters Art Guild, succeeding his father in that capacity. Also a talented artist, Don Swann, Jr., is best known for his etching of "The Old Curiosity Shop."